_ition_

**Illinois Central College**
**Learning Resource Center**

THEODORE CLEVENGER, JR.

*The University of Texas*

# Audience analysis

The Bobbs-Merrill Company, Inc.

A SUBSIDIARY OF HOWARD W. SAMS & CO., INC.

PUBLISHERS    INDIANAPOLIS   NEW YORK   KANSAS CITY

# Editor's foreword

Professor Clevenger has written a contemporary book in the sense that audience analysis is a significant facet of a new American malaise. Today the underdeveloped world still faces problems of starvation; Europe and Russia must develop economies that can meet consumer demands generated by the revolution of expectations of the last one hundred years. America is faced with a different problem, the problem of an economic system that produces more goods than the effective consumers in the system can reasonably use. The problem suggests two obvious answers: Create more consumers by converting the poor into active consumers; create greater needs among existing consumers. The federal government has apparently opted for the first solution; private enterprise for the second.

In practice, the attempt to create consumers has resulted in a multiplication of communications designed to persuade. This attempt to manipulate thought and behavior is reinforced by American cultural habits. The nature of a free society has, since colonial times, encouraged spokesmen for both religion and government to employ communication as social control. Now, however, commerce has joined church and state, and the advertisement or commercial has joined sermon and stump speech as persuasion for social control.

If persuasion has become a felt necessity of the economic system, then the methods of persuasion have become increasingly more sophisticated and subtle with the explosion of our knowledge of propaganda. This marriage of need and knowledge has produced at least two effects. The first is obvious—a multiplication of exposure to persuasive communications. The second, less apparent, is the new American malaise—the fear of manipulation, the nightmare that while we have gained the world we have lost our souls to anonymous controllers of thought and mind. This malaise is expressed in our attitudes of condescension; it is also expressed in our admiration of Madison Avenue apparent in phrases like "the hidden persuaders" and "subliminal persuasion"; it is expressed in the popularity of **Brave New World,** which may represent our fear of manipulation raised to the power of a delirious apparition.

Professor Clevenger directs himself in this book at the new persuasion, since the key to it is "audience analysis." This analysis rests squarely on the subjects discussed here: opinion research, statistical analysis, thought and belief systems, the effects of communication, a strategy of communication. These concepts "suggest beginning points and general frameworks for audience analysis in a variety of communications situations." These "general frameworks" move us toward an understanding of modern persuasion by helping to teach the ways in which people are influenced in our society. They suggest that most of the attempts to affect our attitudes and opinions are based on careful thought, elaborate examinations of public opinion, careful pretesting of sample audiences, the scholarly study of belief systems and learning theory.

A knowledge of the processes of mass persuasion illuminates an important part of our culture and would make this study worthwhile in itself. Beyond this, however, Professor Clevenger's presentation is aimed at the person who wishes to persuade. This fact is not to suggest that Professor Clevenger wants to run with the hare and hunt with the hounds. We can learn that some appeals are essentially unethical, that they attempt to convince in irrational ways. Thus may a soap commercial suggest a return to virginity or the carefree eroticism of adolescence. By knowing the bases of these kinds of appeal, we can realize how we ought not to be persuaded. Out of the same knowledge and insight can come the knowledge and insight of how to persuade rationally and ethically.

As this book points out, all appeals are based on choices. These choices should be made on the basis of information and analysis. Thus the speaker should utilize theories of audience analysis to make choices relating to audience selection, message planning, message pretesting, and monitoring of effects. By being made aware of the tools and guidelines by which wise decisions on these matters can be made, the speaker becomes both a more effective and a more responsible persuader. This is to say, at best, that the speaker will become more helpful to his audience—that by speaking relevantly he will help his auditors make better decisions about controversies significant to them.

In short, **Audience Analysis** hopes to make the student familiar both with what the best speakers have known by intuition about audiences and what behavioral science is organizing and proving about audiences. Such knowledge is indispensable both to the would-be persuader and to the citizen who cannot escape mass persuasion in his daily living.

**Russel R. Windes**

# Contents

## 2. Some general approaches to audiences

## LIST OF FIGURES

# Preface

This book grew out of a series of lectures for an upper-division undergraduate course in audience analysis offered at U.C.L.A. during the summer of 1964.

The class was small but articulate, and the prepared lectures generally were followed by vigorous class discussion. Whatever clarity and force the following chapters may have is due in no small part to the impact of this creative interchange.

That impact was substantial. Of the original twelve lectures, two that proved less useful than expected have been left out of this book. The remaining ten have been revised extensively and reorganized into the seven chapters that follow. In a sense, then, this book has something of the character of a second edition, revised, supplemented, and condensed in answer to responses of a small but able sample of its target audience.

This volume is intended primarily for the undergraduate who is interested in the process of speech communication and especially in the usually silent but ultimately crucial participant in that process, the auditor. The auditor is described in terms that are for the most part easily grasped by an intelligent freshman or sophomore. Where it is necessary to use language that might be unfamiliar to such a reader, terms are defined. Consequently, this book probably will find its widest use in a basic college or university speech course. Much of the content, however, deals with concepts that traditionally have been reserved for more advanced courses. Therefore, it is possible to use this book, augmented by extensive supplementary readings, as the central core of an advanced course.

It is hoped that the student will gain from the following chapters an enlarged understanding of what the auditor is like, how he can respond to communication, and what factors interact to shape his response. Nowhere will the reader find a recipe telling him step-by-step "How to Analyze an Audience"; instead, he will be asked to consider certain concepts, facts, and relations, which, hopefully, he may find interesting and valuable in their own right whether or not he ever intends to do an audience analysis. If he should be of a more pragmatic turn of mind, he may use these as a basis for constructing a variety of procedures of his own to fit the circumstances of present or future communication situations; but my intent is to describe, not to advise.

I owe a large debt of gratitude for contributions of many kinds to the writing of this book:

To Waldo Phelps, chairman of the Department of Speech at U.C.L.A., for inviting me to teach the course which led to the development of these ideas.

To my students, for the creative responses that have shaped my thinking.

To Russel Windes, for his patient and helpful editorial supervision.

To Mrs. Elizabeth Ann Magasano and Mrs. Kay Davenport, for typing and other essential secretarial services.

To my wife, Charlotte, for that perfect blend of generous support and incisive criticism that kept me, throughout various stages of revision, balanced between the Scylla of overconfidence and the Charybdis of despair.

To Ted, Ruth, Ricky, and Libby, for understanding how to manage a father who is writing a book.

*Part one*

# THE BASES OF AUDIENCE ANALYSIS

# ONE

# The audience in speech communication

## *An audience-centered approach to communication*

Because of the central role it plays in society, spoken communication has been an object of interest, speculation, and intensive study for thousands of years. It has been analyzed in many ways and discussed from every imaginable point of view. However, by granting a bit of latitude for generalization, this great variety may be reduced to four broad avenues of approach to the subject, all of which may be seen to fit into a single, coherent map of the speech-communication process.

**The process of speech communication.** In a highly simplified view of the process, speech communication consists of a speaker transmitting a message to a listener. Of course, some analyses of communication devote more attention to one aspect of this sequence of events than to the others, and some analyses provide a much more detailed picture of the entire process than this provides. Most well-developed views of speech communication, however, recognize each of the four entities mentioned in the foregoing statement: the speaker, the listener, the message, and the transmission process. This over-all sketch of what happens in communication provides the framework into which may be fit four distinctive approaches to the study of communication.

3

**Focus on the speaker.** Although speaker-centered approaches to communication differ in many ways from one another, all focus on the speaker as the most important element in the communicative situation.

One such approach considers the speaker's purposes and how they may best be accomplished, and so may be characterized as a **pragmatic** or instrumental view of oral communication. Another approach is essentially **moralistic** in that it seeks to evaluate from an ethical standpoint the speaker's goals and the techniques by which he works toward them. A third speaker-centered approach, arising out of the **behavioral** viewpoint, calls for an understanding of what the speaker does and why he does it. Still another approach is more difficult to classify because it seems to incorporate elements of each of the other three approaches blended with some considerations of esthetics and social propriety. This fourth approach may perhaps best be classified as the **good-speech** approach, for it is concerned with what the speaker must do in order to speak well; that is, to speak in accordance with generally accepted standards of good speech.

Each of these approaches is different; yet each shares with the others a primary emphasis on the speaker. The other elements in the communicative process, especially listener and message, are taken into account, but largely because they shed additional light on the speaker's function.

**Focus on the message.** Message-oriented approaches to speech communication focus on the speech as the primary object of consideration.

A **stylistic** approach, for instance, considers such topics as word choice, sentence structure, and figurative language, and seeks to understand the verbal and other ingredients of which speeches (or other messages) are composed. An **idea-critical** approach, on the other hand, ignores style and concentrates on the speaker's ideas, evaluating them with reference to their acceptability, appropriateness, or their value in dealing with contemporary problems. A third approach is found in **content analysis,** which may deal with either ideas or style, but which usually describes the topics the speaker talked about, the attitudes he expressed, and the relative emphasis he placed upon one topic or attitude as opposed to another. A fourth message-oriented approach to communication is found in applied **logic**. A speech (either one contemplated or one actually delivered) may be analyzed from the standpoint of its logical structure: whether propositions are supported with appropriate evidence, whether certain important premises are suppressed, and whether conclusions flow logically from the propositions advanced to support them.

These four approaches, which together make up only a small sample of the great variety of message-oriented approaches to communication, differ greatly but are alike in their preoccupation with the message as the focal point in the communicative process.

**Focus on transmission.** Messages do not flow directly from the mind of the speaker to the mind of the listener. They must be transmitted from one to the other by some physical means. Several approaches to speech communication focus on this transmission process, of which we shall consider two representative examples.

The **phonetic** approach is concerned with the individual sounds used by a language as a vehicle of transmission. It is concerned with the physiological conformations of throat and mouth that produce the distinctive speech sounds, with the sound-wave patterns which characterize each, and with the processes by means of which the sounds are recognized and distinguished from one another. A second transmission-centered approach is represented by **information theory.** The most highly mathematical of all the communication sciences, information theory seeks ways of measuring and expressing quantitatively the capacity of a language to transmit information and the rate at which information can be passed through communication channels in various forms and under various conditions.

To a certain extent each of these approaches, the phonetic and the information theory, takes the speaker and the listener into account; but whenever they do so it is generally in order to achieve a fuller understanding of the transmission process.

**Focus on the listener.** Of all the approaches to oral communication, few treat the listener as the primary focus of attention. Not doing so is entirely understandable, for the listener is neither the most overtly active nor the most easily studied feature of the communicative process. Despite the listener's apparent passivity and the difficulties that audiences present as an object of study, it is possible to make an audience-centered approach to communication. In order to distinguish this approach from the other three, we shall notice three audience-centered approaches to communication.

Before they are put on the air, new television shows are sometimes tested by a technique known as **program analysis**, which represents an audience-centered approach to the selection of broadcast material. A test group of auditors, selected for its similarity to some "target" audience, is exposed to segments of the new program. As the auditor views the broadcast he continuously registers his reactions on a special recording device. Later these recorded reactions are analyzed in order to estimate the target audience's preferences for various kinds of program content. Broadcasters use such procedures to build a picture of the audience's patterns of taste.

A quite different audience-centered viewpoint is represented by the **listening** approach. Although we spend far more time listening than we do speaking, it is curiously true that we spend far more time studying the art of speaking than we do studying the art of listening. In an effort to remedy this situation, books have been written and courses of study instituted that attempt to teach the art of effective, purposeful listening.

Finally, educators and social psychologists have become interested in what listeners do after they have been exposed to instruction or propaganda. Message-centered and speaker-centered approaches have always been interested in the immediate responses of listeners, but more with a view to understanding how speeches achieve their effect (or how best to advise speakers) rather than with a view to understanding how the listener functions. These more recent **audience-effect studies** represent a subtle shift of interest. The listener in these studies becomes the primary focus, and the important questions become: (1) What is it about the listener that causes a given message to have a particular effect? (2) What are the mechanisms within the listener that govern such matters as forgetting and deterioration of persuasive effect? (3) How does the way in which the listener interacts with others after exposure to the speech determine the long-range effects of the speech?

These and many related considerations form the subject matter of this book. We shall have to be concerned at times with speakers, messages, and the transmission process; for it is impossible to deal comprehensively with any aspect of communication without occasionally taking the other aspects into account. But our focus will always be upon the listener. That is, whenever we consider any other aspect of the communication process, it will be with a view to using that information to further our understanding of what the listener is like, what he does in the communication situation, and what are its effects upon him.

## Auditor and audience

Of the many difficulties involved in an audience-centered approach to communication perhaps the most troublesome is the need to preserve the distinction between the auditor (the individual listener) and the audience (the collection of listeners). The distinction is easily obscured, but failure to maintain it leads to vagueness, ambiguity, confusion, and eventually to erroneous ideas. We shall first outline some considerations that are important from the standpoint of auditors, then present some important features of audiences.

**Auditors.** Any analysis of individual auditors must begin with the recognition that listening is behavior. It is an ancient and obvious truism—but one often overlooked—that listening is not a passive activity. Even the most relaxed and effortless sort of listening, such as one might give in response to music, light drama, or a humorous after-dinner talk, involves doing something. In certain instances, superficial analysis may give the impression that the listener, though undergoing changes and hence "active" in that sense of the word, is in reality a "passive" instrument in the hands of a skilled communicator who activates desired responses in the listener by administering the correct sequence of stimuli. However, more detailed examination reveals a very different picture, one in which the listener plays a much more active role in determining both the nature and the outcome of the communicative encounter. The auditor is involved in a continuous sequence of behavior, only some of which is under the apparent control of the speaker. Much of the presumed audience control of skillful public speakers resides not so much in their ability to manipulate audiences as in their adroitness at fitting their speeches to ongoing behavioral patterns and tendencies in the audience. Viewed from this standpoint, the behavior of the audience may have as great an influence upon the speaker as his behavior has upon the audience. But regardless of the net balance of influence, it is clear that listening, like all other human activity, consists of the behavior of individuals.

Because listening is behavior, it is governed by the same principles that govern all other behavior. The total constellation of factors influencing such complex behaviors as often arise in the speaking-listening situation is not completely understood, but it is clear that several levels and types of learning are involved. Although the point has not been fully proved, it is a good working hypothesis that whatever people do in any situation (including the listening situation) will be consistent with what they have learned to do both in that situation and in other situations that they think to be relevant to it. Furthermore, until we have convincing evidence to the contrary, it seems sensible to presume that the individual does not change basically when cast in the role of auditor; that is, what he does as a listener grows out of the same habits, values, beliefs, and motives that serve as references for his behavior in other settings.

To suggest that the same factors that control an individual's listening behavior also control his other behaviors is to imply that he brings to the listening situation all of his previous experience. In other words, how an individual responds on a given occasion is a product of the stimuli of the moment as interpreted in the light of his life history. Of course, not every previous experience will be relevant to any given moment's behavior; but even the question of which experiences are relevant is determined by perceptions, habits, values, and so forth, which are themselves products of experience, and hence individual. The point is that the auditor brings much more than some imaginary and universal "listening faculty" to the communicative setting; he enters the setting as an individual whole and entire, bringing the residue of his whole life's experience with him.

To say that the individual comes to the listening situation with all of his prior experience at hand is not to imply that he will respond uniformly to the same message in every situation. Quite the reverse is true, for part of his experience will have taught him to discriminate among a very great variety of different contexts. An isolated stimulus occurring in one context may elicit from him a very different response from that elicited by the same stimulus occurring in a different context. Among all his responses, these rules of context play a particularly important role, and often account for apparent inconsistencies in behavior. Most people are able to distinguish among many different situations in which they are receivers of communications. In each of these situations a slightly different set of perceptions and response tendencies may be called forth. To some stimuli the individual will respond uniformly in all of these discriminably different contexts; but other stimuli will lead to responses that differ markedly from one context to another. Again it is important to emphasize that "context" is here determined by the individual; two sets of circumstances that represent essentially identical contexts for one person may represent quite different contexts for another.

Any attempt to understand auditors must be guided by the recognition that listening is behavior; that as behavior it is controlled by the same principles that govern other types of behavior; that the auditor interprets an incoming message within the framework of his prior experience; and that this interpretation will be carried out under whatever rules of context the individual auditor has learned to apply in communication situations.

**Audiences.** The definition of the term "audience" has received far more attention than it deserves. Unfortunately, efforts to formulate a proper definition of the term have resulted in the labeling of certain groups with a particular set of characteristics as "audiences" and the excluding of all other groups of auditors. These other groups are then called "mobs," "small groups," "crowds," "aggregations," or the like, and are excluded as objects of audience analysis.

To distinguish between audiences on one hand and various kinds of nonaudience listening groups on the other, though pointless, is not inherently harmful; but this distinction may lead to serious confusion if it causes us to believe that entirely different principles operate in one situation as opposed to the others. Each individual in a group behaves as he does because of his prior experience coupled with the stimuli operating upon him at the moment, including the context as he perceives it. Because experiences, contexts, and stimuli control behavior, and because they are almost infinitely variable, it is a great oversimplification to label some groups "audiences," other groups "crowds" or "mobs," and so on. When we look closely at what individuals do in groups, we discover not just a

few different types of groups, as these ordinary labels imply, but
very many different types that differ from one another in a variety
of ways. Therefore, it is more profitable to concentrate attention
upon those variables that influence the behavior of people in groups
than to allow our thinking to be controlled by the popular labels
that presumably distinguish one type of group from another.

In accordance with the foregoing thoughts, we will ordinarily use
the term "audience" to refer to a group of auditors who either are
or might be listening to a given message at a particular time. We
will use the term flexibly. Sometimes it will be convenient to use it
more broadly; for instance, to refer to several groups who hear the
speech at different times. Sometimes we will need to use it more
narrowly; for instance, to refer to some subgroup contained within
a larger group hearing a particular speech. However, we will never
use the term "audience" to set apart a particular type or sort of
auditor group to be distinguished from nonaudiences. We shall not
regard "the audience" as something mysterious or unique; it is
simply the shorthand term we shall employ to refer to a collection
of actual or potential auditors for a particular speech or other
message.

Even though we regard it as trivial to distinguish between audiences and nonaudiences, many of the characteristics that are sometimes used to make such distinctions are themselves significant
audience characteristics. A review of the distinctions sometimes
mentioned in the definition of "audience" will emphasize some important features that distinguish some audiences from others.

An important audience characteristic in most of the situations
with which we are here concerned is **plurality;** that is, there is more
than one listener who must be taken into account. Of course,
speech communication takes place in groups of every size, ranging
from situations involving a single listener to those involving many
millions of listeners. However, whenever two or more listeners are
jointly present they become part of the communication context and
a source of stimuli for one another. As we shall see later, this
stimulation may either simplify or complicate the structure of the
communication situation; but in any case, it changes it.

Moreover, the **size** of the audience is a factor that may influence
the way in which auditors respond (and hence how they influence
one another). Sources and patterns of stimulation that appear to
have a profound influence upon response in most very large audi-

ences often have a contrary influence or none at all in smaller audiences, and vice versa.

To some extent the influence of audience size is in turn affected by two other variables. One of these is **homogeneity,** the extent to which members of the group share a common background of experience, attitudes, habits of thought, and other common traits. As we will see later, most groups of individuals assembled together have at least some things in common with one another (otherwise they would be unlikely to assemble); but the type and extent of similarity differs greatly from one audience to another. In trying to understand how a given audience behaves, we will find it important to consider what and how much its members have in common.

A second factor affecting the influence of audience size is **group feeling,** the extent to which the members of the audience are aware of and responding to one another. Feelings of "togetherness" may be strong or weak in various members of an audience; an auditor under the influence of strong feelings of group togetherness responds to the others around him and to the stimuli presented by a speech quite differently than if he felt less involved.

**Orderliness** is a characteristic that is frequently used to separate audiences from less well-regulated crowds. The fact is, however, that no clear-cut distinction can be made between "orderly" audiences on one hand and "disorderly" crowds on the other; auditor groups vary along a continuum ranging from near-absolute conformity at one end to nearly total randomness at the other, and there is no tendency for them to fall into two neatly defined categories.

One factor that contributes to orderliness in an audience is the condition known as **preliminary tuning;** that is, a state of readiness to respond to some particular person or thing in a uniform and predictable fashion. For instance, patriotic music is sometimes played or sung at a political rally in the expectation that it will produce a particular type of preliminary tuning in the audience; that is, the sponsors hope that following such music most auditors will be in a state of heightened readiness to respond to patriotic speeches. The concept of preliminary tuning takes note of a certain inertia in auditors' moods and thought patterns. Once auditors have been channeled into a particular train of thought or emotion, subsequent stimuli related to that thought or emotion elicit from them stronger and more uniform responses than would otherwise be the case. Obviously an audience in which all or most of the auditors are "tuned" to a state of readiness to respond in a similar fashion is quite different in character from an audience in which each auditor has a different response readiness.

A common response readiness in a group of auditors will be neither established nor maintained unless they have a **common focus of attention.** A crowd in an airport lobby, for instance, typically displays a great many different focuses of attention; that is, everybody is paying attention to something different. On the other hand, the crowd at a boxing match usually shares a common focus of attention to an unusually high degree. Attention in a group of auditors may change focus many times during the course of a few minutes. In the airport lobby attention focuses from time to time on the voice of the dispatch clerk announcing arrivals and departures, only to dissipate again when his announcement is over; between rounds at a prize fight the attention of the crowd dissipates into hundreds of individual focuses only to refocus on the ring when the bell announces the beginning of another round. The people in any audience are, of course, paying attention to something all of the time; but we speak of their attention as focused only when most of them are attending to the same stimuli simultaneously. It is probably inaccurate ever to say that the audience at a public speech is not paying attention, for each auditor is certainly attending to something, regardless of how many or few are attending to the speech.

Closely related to the single focus of attention is an audience condition that has been called **polarization.** Generally speaking, the term refers to the existence of two opposing and complementary states. An electric battery, for example, is polarized; it has a positive and a negative terminal, one of which repels and the other of which attracts free electrons. As applied to audiences, the term refers to the listeners' acceptance of the speaker as occupying a role that is opposite and complementary to their own; an audience is polarized when its members assume a listening attitude and regard the speaker as separate and apart from their own situation. When the auditors have a conscious acceptance of the speaker as speaker and themselves as listeners, the audience is said to be polarized. Clearly an audience composed of individuals who have taken on the polar role of "listeners" and cast some speaker in the polar role of "speaker" would respond to different stimuli more readily than would an audience composed of unpolarized individuals. Moreover, such an audience will be likely, though by no means certain, to share a single focus of attention upon the speaker a greater proportion of the time.

When auditors come together in groups, they influence one another's responses, with the nature and extent of the influence depending upon such factors as audience size, homogeneity, group feeling, orderliness, preliminary tuning, common focus, and polarization. A group of auditors need not be large, homogeneous, possessed of group feeling, orderly, preliminarily tuned, sharing a common focus of attention, or polarized in order to qualify as an audience; but all of these variables are important in distinguishing among different audience situations that lead to different patterns of audience response.

## The audience as a statistical concept

Even though we use the term "the audience" as if it referred to a single entity, the term has little meaning as a unitary concept, for it does not describe a single, individual thing. But the singular (rather than plural) form of the noun "audience" predisposes speakers of English to think of audiences as wholes. The resulting confusion is further heightened by the similarity of usage between this noun and other collective nouns such as "flock" and "herd." When we say that "the flock has moved out to pasture" or "the herd is now across the river," we state something that is true of every single animal in the flock or herd; but when we say that "the audience was deeply moved" we are doing nothing of the kind, and when we say that a particular speaker addressed "an audience of students from various liberal groups on campus" we use the term "audience" in a very different way indeed. Sometimes, to be sure, the members of an audience will react so similarly that they can, for all practical purposes, be regarded as a faceless flock or herd of essentially identical persons who move together as a coherent whole; but this is a very special case. Usually we must be prepared to account for diversity in both audience make-up and audience response.

This diversity represents individual differences. We have observed that experiences, values, context, perceptions, and other determinants of behavior are individual, just as behavior itself is individual. To think clearly about what people do and what leads them to do it, we must think in individual terms.

On the other hand, we have discussed such factors as size, homogeneity, preliminary tuning, and other variables that are clearly related more directly to the group as a whole rather than to the individuals. Furthermore, although we may keep in mind simultaneously the separate ideas, emotions, predispositions, and reactions of a few individual auditors, as audiences increase in size we find it increasingly more difficult to take such detailed individual differences into account. When an assemblage reaches even a moderate size—say fifteen or twenty auditors—coherence requires that we treat them as a group, even though their behavior is individually rather than collectively determined.

This is the dilemma that lies at the very root of audience analysis: We cannot consider independently and at once every single auditor in a large audience; yet we cannot consider the audience as if it were a single auditor. What we require to extricate us from this dilemma is some way of thinking about the audience that will permit us to summarize briefly the similarities and differences among its separate auditors. Our summary can then be regarded as a shorthand description, which tells us how things are typically or on the average in the audience as a whole. We must bear in mind that such a summary description may tell us nothing about any individual auditor; yet, if we take each individual equally into account in summarizing, then each will be represented in equal measure in the summary.

**The statistical viewpoint.** The idea of assembling a large amount of information about individuals into manageable form is essentially a statistical concept. Tables, distribution graphs, percentages, averages, and other statistical techniques summarize great quantities of information about many individuals in such a way that it is possible to make general statements about the group. The same amount of information, if not considered statistically, would lead only to confusion.

Consider, for example, the following illustration. A group of 28 college students about to hear a speech on diplomatic recognition of Communist China were asked to express their attitudes toward the proposition on an 11-point scale. Each student registered his opinion by choosing the number between "1" and "11" that best expressed his feelings on the subject: a response of "1" indicated a position strongly favoring recognition; a response of "11" indicated a position strongly opposing recognition; a response of "6" indicated a neutral or undecided position. The students gave the following 28 responses:

> 7, 2, 4, 10, 3, 5, 9, 1, 11, 2, 5, 8, 3, 4, 10, 9, 1, 2, 5, 9, 1, 3, 3, 2, 8, 4, 4, 3.

What was the attitude of this audience toward recognition of Communist China? Each potential auditor responded differently, and examining the responses one-by-one it appears that we could say nothing about the attitudes of this audience. However, by making a distribution graph of the responses, an interesting and informative picture of audience attitudes emerges from the formerly confusing individual differences. The twenty-eight student responses are plotted in Figure 1, where the abscissa represents the eleven possible scale responses and the ordinate represents the number of students selecting each response.

*Figure 1. Attitudes of 28 Students Toward Recognition of Communist China*

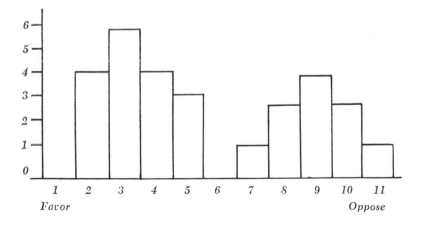

By resorting to statistical concepts, it is possible to say that prior to the speech this audience was composed of two different groups, a small group opposed to recognition and a larger group favoring it.

Attitudes were rather moderate, however, with few extreme responses in either direction and with the "modal" or commonest attitudes concentrated at the mildly favorable and mildly unfavorable positions. There was no well-defined group of neutrals, though some of the students with favorable attitudes and some with unfavorable attitudes were virtually neutral.

This statistical description provided by the distribution graph and its interpretation tells us little about any individual member of the group. On the other hand, each individual is represented in equal measure with all others. Using such techniques as these, we do not lose sight of the individuals, even though we do not focus upon them individually. The individual auditor's attitude in this case is not "lost" in the statistical treatment; rather, it is placed in a context relative to the attitudes of the other auditors, and the shape of the over-all pattern of responses serves to describe an important aspect of the audience.

To the extent that it is helpful in understanding response to communication, the concept "the audience" refers to over-all patterns of the characteristics and responses of auditors. In short, "the audience" is a statistical concept. When we speak of the characteristics of an audience, we are talking about the shared, the average, or the typical characteristics of the auditors who compose it.

As we have already noted, we must remember that, although we may describe the group by summarizing individual traits, we cannot reverse the process and describe specific individuals in terms of group traits. Sometimes this is perfectly obvious; for instance, in a group that is 60 per cent male and 40 per cent female, there cannot be an auditor who is 60 per cent one and 40 per cent the other. In other cases it is less obvious but equally true that summary statements about the audience almost never characterize the individual auditor. In the attitude example described by Figure 1, for instance, the **average** attitude is 4.93; yet this figure does not represent the attitudes of most of the students in a way that is at all satisfactory or helpful. In an audience with an average income of $9,437.52 per year there may be no single auditor with that income, and in an audience with an average of 10.7 years formal education there will almost certainly be no single individual with just that much education. These examples underscore the danger of overgeneralizing, even from reliable data. The generalizations about the group do not necessarily apply to most of the individuals in the group.

For this reason, we need to characterize audiences in such a way that we may speak meaningfully of certain characteristics of the group as a whole while at the same time retaining an awareness of individual differences. Such characterization is the essence of the statistical point of view.

Because the statistical mode of thinking permits us to simplify and deal cogently with what would otherwise constitute a complex and bewildering tangle of individual differences, we will find it convenient to approach the audience as an abstraction of an essentially statistical nature. A part of this approach must be our awareness that it is better, whenever possible, to consider auditors rather than the audience; and therefore we must make every effort to keep our generalizations about the audience in touch with their only basis in reality—the characteristics and behaviors of the individual auditors. It is possible to use statistics so as to frustrate this contact between abstractions about "the audience" and the facts about "auditors"; but this is true of every form of generalization, statistical as well as purely verbal. As we shall see, a statistical approach has certain advantages when it comes to recognizing individual differences.

**Rudimentary techniques.** The most elementary statistical methods are so much a part of our daily lives that they are familiar to almost everybody. They are the techniques we use to describe proportion, average, and diversity: percentage, mean, median, mode, range, and frequency distribution. By noticing some of the ways in which these rudimentary statistical techniques apply to audience description, we may come to a fuller understanding of what is meant by the statement that "the audience" is essentially a statistical concept.

Before doing so, however, we should notice that such essentially quantitative concepts as "percentage" and "frequency distribution" have their counterparts in the less exact language of everyday discourse, and indeed grew out of the necessity in commerce and science for expressing with precision the ideas that are imprecisely expressed in common language. Thus, without resorting to quantitative techniques, we rely daily upon quasi-quantitative concepts which are based upon ideas of frequency and degree but which do not specify these exactly; and without conscious recognition that we are doing so, we sometimes draw conclusions from observations in a way that is very similar to statistical summarization.

For example, when a newspaper reports that an audience "applauded wildly" following a political speech, it is reporting a general impression based upon a process of abstraction that is similar to statistical summary. "The audience," being an abstraction, did not applaud; the auditors did—and no doubt there were some auditors who did not applaud wildly, others who applauded even more wildly than the average auditor did, and still others who did not applaud at all. The "wild applause" was an over-all effect; but because it is cumbersome to report what each auditor did, the newspaper reported for "the audience" that behavior which characterized most of its members.

Words such as "some," "many," "few," "all," "often," "mostly," "usually," and similar terms are used widely in ordinary language to express frequency, proportion, degree, and typicality. The frequency with which these words occur in discourse of every kind testifies to the need we have to generalize beyond the individual case and to talk about multiple observations in terms of their shared characteristics and qualities rather than dealing with them as isolated objects and events. In other words, quasi-quantitative and quasi-statistical concepts are an essential part of the way we think and talk about virtually every aspect of the world about us. When we talk about audiences, there is some advantage to recognizing the essentially statistical and quantitative underpinnings of these notions.

Let us consider the case of a speech on birth control. The speaker will probably wish to know whether there are any Catholics in his audience, and how many. Of course, if he is talking to the Knights of Columbus or the Southern Baptist Convention, he will have no difficulty. He will probably be addressing all Catholics in the one case and all non-Catholics in the other, but in most speaking situations he will have to deal with a religiously mixed audience. Whether the speaker in such an instance should consider the religion of his auditors, and in particular whether he should alter his message in any way depending upon the make-up of the audience, is a question that we shall reserve until the next chapter. For now it is enough to note that if we are to understand the audience's response to whatever speech is made on this topic we must know the proportion of Catholic auditors.

It may be enough in this instance to know that "most" of the audience is Catholic, or that "few" auditors are Catholic, or that "about half" are; but such terms do not mean the same things to everyone. Where, in this set of terms, does 60 per cent fall? Is it "most" or "about half"? Is 15 per cent "few" or "some" or "almost none"? The point we must note is that the crucial concept in such instances is proportion, and proportion is most accurately and unambiguously expressed as **percentage.** Whenever we use such proportional terms as "few" or "most," we refer to an underlying continuum of percentages.

*Figure 2. Number of children per Auditor (Mode 0)*

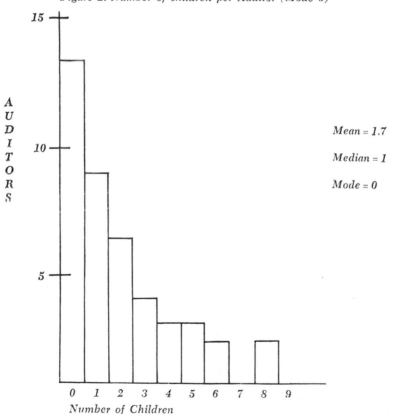

To anticipate the responses of the audience to a speech on birth control, it might also be useful to know how many children each of the auditors has in his or her family. Because we cannot consider each auditor separately, our first thought may be to look for some "average" or "typical" number of children per auditor. One approach is to calculate the **mean** number of children per family represented by the auditors. If every family had either two, three, or four children, and the mean were around three, then this average might be considered a good representation of the audience as a whole. An average is informative and useful if most of the values used to calculate it fall fairly close to the average itself. However, a few families in the audience with seven or eight children or many families with none at all would result in an average that was seriously out of keeping with the actual distribution of children among the members of the audience. In Figures 2 and 3, for example, the means of 1.7 and 4.9 children respectively represent the groups very badly.

Another approach to obtaining a representative number of children per auditor would be to locate the **median.** This is the number that exactly separates the half of the audience with the most children from the half of the audience with the fewest. The advantage

*Figure 3. Number of children per Auditor (Modes 2, 8)*

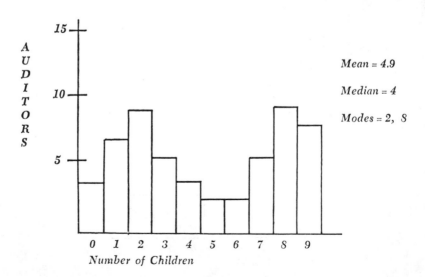

Mean = 4.9

Median = 4

Modes = 2, 8

Number of Children

of the median over the mean in some instances is that the median is not influenced by extreme values. If, for example, we were to add one auditor with sixteen children to the group represented in Figure 2, the mean would jump from about 1.7 to around 2.1, but the median would not be affected at all. Like the mean, the median is most valuable when most of the observations lie close to the average.

Still another approach to obtaining a representative number of children per auditor would be to locate the **mode.** This is the number that occurs most commonly. In Figure 2, the mode is 0. Figure 3 shows a distribution with two modes, one at 2 and the other at 8. The mode in Figure 2 characterizes a group coming from predominantly very small families; the modes in Figure 3 characterize a group having two subgroups contained within it, a small-family subgroup and a very-large-family subgroup.

In Figure 2, neither the mean of approximately 1.7, the median of 1, nor the mode of 0 gives much useful information about the distribution of children among the members of the group. In Figure 3, the mean of 4.9 and the median of 4 are misleading, although the modes of 2 and 8 are fairly representative of the two subgroups within the audience. Statistical techniques take into account the possibility that in a particular group there may be no representative "average" or "typical" case and provide additional approaches that make possible a more detailed view of audience characteristics than is provided by the calculation of "averages" and the location of "typical" auditors.

The danger of distortion arising from misinterpretation of the median, mean, and mode could be reduced by resorting to the essentially statistical idea of dispersion. In the instances under consideration, dispersion is most easily represented by the **range.** The range is the distance between the largest and the smallest number of children. In Figure 2, the range is 0–8; in Figure 3, it is 0–9. When, for Figure 2, we report a mean of 1.7, a median of 1, a mode of 0, and a range from 0 to 8, we know that the auditors must be grouped heavily in the small family categories, with a scattering of larger families represented.

The detailed picture of this "scattering" of larger families may be a matter of no importance. However, if it is important, then the more detailed picture can be obtained from a **frequency distribu-**

**tion.** In the present instance, this is a table or graph showing the frequency with which families of each succeeding size are represented in the audience. Figures 1, 2, and 3 are all frequency distribution graphs. The advantage of the frequency distribution is that it permits one to identify quickly both majority and minority trends in the audience, to locate both typical and unusual cases, and to note the dispersion of auditors with respect to the trait under consideration.

We have taken brief note of a few rudimentary statistical techniques: (1) the percentage, to characterize proportion; (2) the mean and median, to characterize averages in the sense of "central tendency"; (3) the mode, to characterize averages in the sense of "typical case"; (4) the range and the frequency distribution, to characterize dispersion. Whenever we wish to speak precisely about "the audience" we will have to resort to these and other statistical techniques. However, even when we speak imprecisely and generally about "the audience," we will do well to recognize that we are talking about an abstraction that is related to the characteristics of auditors only through the essentially statistical concepts of proportion, central tendency, typicality, and dispersion. The latter is especially important, for it serves to remind us that in most important ways auditors are not all the same.

# TWO

# Planning for speech communication

In most informal and routine communication situations our language behavior is more or less habitual and we seldom pause to consider either purpose or means in utterance. That is, most of the time we do not reflect much upon why we are speaking in a given situation or whether our language is well calculated to obtain any desired end—fortunately, for if we had to plan each utterance in detail like a production schedule or a military campaign, we seldom would get anything said. Whether we consider speech communication from the standpoint of the individual speaker or from the viewpoint of society as a whole, routinization and habit are needed for efficiency.

Occasionally, however, we encounter situations that are not routine; that is, situations for which our customary language habits do not provide an appropriate way of speaking. Sometimes these non-routine situations are so important that we are willing to spend extra effort to guarantee effectiveness. On such occasions we are inclined to consider just what we hope to accomplish by a given utterance and to calculate the most likely means of accomplishing it. In other words, we are likely to formulate a strategy of communication.

Strategic planning often is done for important interpersonal contacts such as the job interview, the sales meeting, or the press conference. In particular, because they usually call for long utterances and have important consequences, most of the situations that we refer to as "public speaking" call for advance planning.

Of course, not every speech calls for planning. For example, in public discussions, there are almost always one or two participants whose sole purpose in speaking is to be heard in public. The primary goal of their utterance is public utterance itself; their speaking is **consummatory**—it is gratifying in itself without respect to its intended or actual effect upon any of the auditors. The only strategy required in this case is some means of getting and holding the floor.

On the other hand, most public speaking is done primarily for some reason other than the gratification of an urge to talk in public; such speaking is **instrumental**—it is done in order to produce some effect upon a group of auditors. Usually before such occasions a speaker is wise to consider his goals and to reflect upon the best way of reaching them.

Sometimes it is impossible to formulate a communication strategy in advance, because the need to communicate arises on the spur of the moment. On other occasions the outcome may not be important enough to warrant the investment of much time and energy in either planning or evaluation. But when the speaker has an instrumental purpose, when there is time to plan and evaluate, and when the outcome of the communication is important, it is advisable to develop some strategy for communication.

To plan intelligently for communication calls for an analysis of the individual or individuals who are to receive it. Audience analysis is interesting in its own right because of the insight which it affords into the process and effects of communication; but it is in the formulation and testing of communication strategy that audience analysis realizes its most widely recognized and most directly practical application.

### Communication strategy

"Communication strategy" means clarifying one's purposes in speaking and settling upon a course of action calculated to fulfil those purposes. Though simple in principle, such a strategy may call for the simultaneous consideration of many factors. Moreover, what factors a speaker takes into account in developing a strategy for a given case will be closely related to the way in which he perceives the total communication situation, and this in turn may depend upon his view of himself, society, and the nature of mankind. Because such "world views" may differ greatly, it is impossible to catalogue all of the possible bases from which communication strategies might be developed. However, most of them are concerned in some way with the standard communication formula of **Who** says **What** to **Whom, When,** and **How,** with what **Effect.** Various approaches to communication strategy place differing emphasis upon the six elements of this formula and take differing views of the elements and their relationships, but all consist of making choices concerning these six matters.

**Elements of the communication formula.** At first glance it may seem that audience analysis is concerned with only one element of this formula, the "to Whom" feature of communication; and audience analysis does focus mainly on this feature. But in planning a communication strategy a speaker cannot dispose of the six elements one at a time. On the contrary, he must take them all into account simultaneously; for each relates to all of the others in the total pattern, so that to view any one element in isolation leads to distortion because it leads to oversimplification. Thus, if we are to understand how audience analysis contributes to communication strategy, we need to consider not just the audience but the other elements of the communication situation as well.

Most of the time we think of the **Who** of the communication formula as a fixed entity, namely the "speaker" who is planning the strategy of communication. In talking about audience analysis, we generally make this assumption, and we think of audience analysis as an aid to that speaker in accomplishing what he desires.

But we need to recognize that the fixed-communicator situation is not representative of all communication, and that in very broad programs of public information or persuasion, the fixed-communicator situation is never the case. Such large programs generally are planned by organizations, agencies, or groups that can obtain the services of many speakers; and here the speaker is a flexible variable. That is, depending upon what specific aspect of the topic is to be discussed or who is to be in the audience, it may appear better to send one rather than another of several available speakers.

Every communication strategy includes some consideration of the message. This is the **What** of the communication formula. In the context of audience analysis, this is the problem of message construction: the selection of content, ideas, and language, and the ordering of these to produce some pattern of probable effects. Usually we assume that the message is the most flexible element in the entire strategy of communication, and in most situations the speaker will spend most of his time and energy planning the speech. But we should not overlook the fact that there are some communication situations that provide a fixed message, and in these cases the primary strategic problem is to find the right audiences and circumstances for the presentation of that message.

The audience is the **Whom** of the communication formula. In developing a strategy of communication, a major task is finding the right audience, describing its characteristics, predicting its responses to communication events, or sometimes observing how auditors respond. It is upon the **Whom** of communication that this book is focused.

The **When** in communication strategy does not refer simply to a certain interval on the calendar or the clock, but to what we usually call "timing" and "context." Two audiences presented with the same message at precisely the same moment may nevertheless differ with respect to "when" they heard the speech if the preceding sequences of other relevant stimuli have been different for the two audiences. Although there is some merit in treating the **When** of communication separately, its primary relevance for our purposes has to do with differences in the auditor from one time and circumstance to another; therefore, in this book we shall treat **When** as an integral part of **Whom.**

Not all ways of presenting a given idea to a particular audience under certain conditions are equally effective. There is also the question of **How** the message is to be presented; that is, through what media. Our focus here will be upon public speaking, but in the formulation of a communication strategy it may be important to consider alternative media. Some types of audience, for example. may be impossible to assemble in a face-to-face situation; other auditors may have little tolerance for public meetings or for extended listening. Some purposes are incompatible with public meetings. For such audiences and purposes, depending upon the message content, it may be more profitable to rely upon newspaper ads, television messages, leaflets, or even door-to-door canvassing. Thus, although the **How** of communication will be treated as a more or less fixed element throughout most of our discussions here, it is well to remember that in many communication situations the question of media selection is one that needs to be taken into account.

Finally there is the question of message **Effect.** In general, we have been taught to think of effects in terms of the speaker's intent. That is, we tend to assume that in planning a strategy of communication our interest in effects is determined by the speaker's purposes. We shall not deal with the general validity of that assumption now, but the reader will have no difficulty recognizing that the speaker may select different purposes with different audiences; that is, his selection of desired effects is sometimes determined partly by his perception of what it is possible to accomplish with a given audience.

**Interrelation of choices.** In discussing the six elements of the communication formula, we have seen that no one of the six is necessarily a fixed value in the public-speaking situation, and that choices concerning all of these six elements enter into the formulation of communication strategies. To appreciate the complexity of these choices, it may be useful to consider the situation in which no one of the six elements is determined in any way, in which no choices have been made. This is a situation of absolute indifference with respect to who will say what to whom, when, and how, with what effect. The possibilities in this situation are infinite; but under these circumstances there is no motivation to speak, and such a situation is not really a communication situation at all.

But now let us make a choice concerning one of the six elements. Let us say that **you** are to be the speaker. Without actually specifying any more than that, we have already reduced the possibilities (or the reasonable ones in any case) from infinity to a relatively small set. Simply by making a choice of speaker, we have ruled out for all practical purposes a wealth of possible combinations of messages, audiences, occasions, and effects that would be possible given some other speaker. Even if we assume for the sake of argument that you could deliver a speech on virtually any topic and could command the attention of practically any audience, still your speech to that audience would have effects quite different from the effects the same speech would have upon that audience if another speaker were to present it. Thus in choosing one element, we have partially determined the other elements as well.

Now let us make still another choice. Suppose we specify that you are to address an audience composed of students enrolled in an undergraduate speech course at a particular institution of higher learning. For all practical purposes we have now eliminated still more combinations, not just combinations of speaker and audience, but combinations of subject, occasion, and effect. For example, will this audience respond favorably to **any** speech in favor of legalizing narcotics? Will they respond favorably to **you** speaking on this topic? Could you teach them about the atomic structure of the interior of the sun? Make them want to read **Tristram Shandy?** Get them to contribute to the campus blood drive? Lead them to speak favorably of Syngman Rhee? Convince them to give up smoking? Could you cause them to feel the awesome grandeur of the Grand Canyon? If you could get them out of the speech class and in another environment, would you be able to do more? Or would they listen to you at all outside the class? As a group, would they assemble to hear anybody out of class?

Despite the limitations placed upon you by these choices of speaker and audience, there are still many messages you can deliver and many effects you can elicit. Suppose, however, that we make one more choice. You are to produce, as the effect of whatever message you present, a positive change in the attitudes of these students toward the Soviet Union. We have now reduced the situation to one in which there are very few additional choices that can be made, for there are relatively few speeches that you can make in speech class to that group of students that will have the effect of producing more positive attitudes toward the USSR. Just how many such messages there are will depend upon who you are, who your auditors are, and what situational factors are at work. It is conceivable that for some combinations of speaker, audience, and circumstances, no such speech can be found—that is, given the other elements in the formula, the desired outcome is impossible. If the outcome is what we most desire, we will then have to change some of the other elements: speaker, audience, or circumstances. But if such a message is possible, audience analysis can help us find it, and if it is impossible, then audience analysis may be able to tell us so.

The preceding example illustrates in a general way what we mean when we say that the development of a communication strategy is complex. A choice with respect to any element in the strategy reduces the possible range of choices concerning the other elements as well, and that is why no choice can be made in isolation. Of course, we have used the word "choice" quite loosely here. Sometimes what we have called a "choice" will simply be a fixed element determined by some aspect of the speaking situation; for instance, the audience is often not chosen but simply given. But the effect is still the same: Whether chosen or given, a particular audience closes some possibilities and opens others.

**Is planning ethical?** It has sometimes been asked whether the formulation of a communication strategy is ethically defensible: Should a speaker plot and scheme concerning how to produce some predetermined effect upon an unsuspecting audience? Wouldn't it be better to just "speak his piece" and let the chips fall where they may? In fact, the word "strategy" in itself suggests a manipulative approach to others, which does not fit comfortably into our concept of free, open, and fair dealings with other people—and audiences are people.

It is especially appropriate at this point to note that the term "strategy" includes choices that have already been made in the communication situation—by others, by circumstances, and by chance—as well as decisions concerning those choices that are still open to the speaker.

It is also important to recognize that, whether he realizes what he is doing or not, the speaker cannot avoid making choices that affect the outcome of communication. Even when a speaker does not consciously take his audience into account, he makes assumptions about them and about the way they will respond to his speaking. At worst, the speaker assumes that his auditors are in the same circumstances as he, and that they will respond to his words and ideas in the same way as he responds to them. After the message has been presented, he may even assume that the audience has in fact responded as he assumed they would. Many bewildering and sometimes unrecognized communication failures grow out of this crude and misleading substitute for audience analysis.

Consider the case of a guest lecturer at a women's club who has been invited to talk about the cultivation of tulips and other early-flowering bulbs. The lecturer has a good deal of information about the subject, but how is she to decide what to present? From an audience-centered viewpoint, she will need to be sure that her auditors have certain basic concepts, and if they do not, she will have to provide them. In order to know whether to talk about basic techniques of cultivation, exotic varieties, or techniques for achieving special effects, she will need to know something about the amount and variety of information her auditors already have. This is the approach she will take if she wishes to plan her communication for maximum effectiveness. On the other hand, she could take the position that she knows what it is important to say about tulip cultivation, and plan her speech without taking the specific audience into account. If she follows the latter course of action, her speech may be a brilliant success if it should by chance match audience knowledge and interests extremely well; but the odds are much better that it would result in little information gain and substantial loss of interest in the topic. Which course of action is more ethical?

Or think about the middle-class social worker who goes into a slum neighborhood to help community leaders there plan a playground. Suppose the social worker assumes that she knows all about playgrounds and their planning, and disdains to learn anything about her auditors. If she regards her auditors as passive receivers of her messages, and if she therefore refuses to take them into account in speaking, she is likely to convey the impression that she really does not understand the problem that the playground is intended to solve, really does not understand the children who are to use the playground, and is really an agent of another culture come to impose its standards and values on people whom it regards as inferior. Probably most of these conclusions will be only partly true and perhaps entirely wrong, but they could have been predicted on the basis of auditor characteristics if the social worker had been willing to consider her auditors. Was her unwillingness to adapt to her audience ethical?

Finally, think of the legislator who wants a particular bill passed because of the good it will do for farmers. The bill also will benefit city consumers and retailers, but the legislator is not as strongly motivated by these considerations as he is by the benefits to farmers. So in addressing city audiences, he presents **his** reasons for adoption, ignoring the benefits to **them**. In permitting his auditors to develop a distorted view of their relation to the bill, due to the differences between their orientation and his, has the legislator followed an ethical course of action?

In short, an accurate assessment of the communication situation, and especially of the audience, may play a significant role in the success of the speech, whether we evaluate success from the standpoint of the speaker's purposes or from the standpoint of how much the audience profited from hearing the speech. Careful planning of communication strategy may contribute as much or more to the realization of the audience's goals as it does to those of the speaker.

We have spoken of communication strategy largely in terms of the planning of a single speech, but it is also possible to consider more elaborate strategies. These may involve several audiences, numerous speakers, several levels of purpose, many speeches, and multiple stages of development. In order to allow for both simple and complex planning, we shall discuss in the next chapter both pre-analysis of audiences and post-testing for the effect of a particular speech.

# THREE

# The function of audience analysis

In the preceding chapter, we spoke of communication strategy largely in terms of planning a single speech, but it is also possible to consider more elaborate strategies. These may involve several audiences, numerous speakers, several levels of purpose, many speeches, and several stages of development. In order to allow for both simple and complex planning, we shall discuss both pre-analysis of audiences and post-testing for the effect of a particular speech.

## Pre-analysis of audiences

Audience analysis enters into strategy most directly at four points: audience selection, message planning, message pretesting, and monitoring of effects.

**Audience selection.** Frequently a speaker is not at liberty to select the groups before which he will appear. Anyone who accepts an invitation to deliver a commencement address or to speak to a businessmen's luncheon or to participate in a TV debate, must work with whatever audience will attend the commencement or the luncheon or will tune in the debate. In these situations the audience (or their representative) has selected the speaker; the speaker may try to find out as much as possible about his audience in order to

32

adapt to their idiosyncrasies, but he must accept them as they are.

To be sure, the speaker may decide that not all of the audience before which he will speak is of interest to him, and that he is concerned only with communicating something of importance to a certain set of auditors within the larger group. At commencement, for example, he may choose to tailor his speech to the graduates; others (parents, teachers, friends) will be present in the audience and will also hear the speech, but the speaker may virtually ignore them and speak to the graduates alone. Or, as important statesmen often do, the speaker may ignore everyone in the immediate audience and tailor his speech for a nationwide audience that will hear, see, or read the speech through the mass media. In either case, the speaker is in effect selecting an audience in the sense that he is tailoring the speech for its impact on some target group, and is treating other groups of auditors as essentially irrelevant eavesdroppers.

Sometimes, though, a speaker is able to select the group or groups that will hear him speak. If his object is to spread information about a particular idea, event, or program, he may consider who would be in the most strategic position to pass the information on to others. By tailoring a message for key groups he may be able to multiply his own efforts through the amplifying effects of these secondary communicators. For this reason, writers, newsmen, and community leaders are considered prime audiences; a word to them under the right circumstances will be enormously amplified through retransmission.

If the speaker's object is to foster adoption of a new idea (whether it be a new variety of seed corn, a new hairdo, or a new program for social welfare) he may find it possible to economize his efforts and reduce the likelihood of mobilizing an opposition by speaking first to people who are more likely to be favorable or open-minded toward changes of the sort he wishes to propose. Depending upon the idea, he may consider it wise to address his initial efforts to the young, the rich, the well-educated, the cosmopolitan, the aspiring, the disenchanted, the desperate, or whatever other group he judges most likely to offer fertile ground for his idea. Of course, if the speaker wishes to address himself to an audience having certain attitudes or characteristics, then it becomes a part of his communication strategy either to find such an audience or to create one. This is not always easy to do, but, where possible, it does increase the likelihood that the idea, when it comes to the attention of a more general public, will bring with it some degree of public support.

The decision to tailor his speech to part of the whole audience or the decision to seek out a particular audience to address cannot be made without considering differences between audiences or groups of auditors. Nor can such decisions be made without considering the relationships between these audience differences and the speaker's topic and purpose. Thus, where choice of audience is a factor in planning a communication strategy, audience analysis plays a vital role.

**Message planning.** The planning of a long verbal message, such as a newspaper story, a television commercial, or a public speech, involves hundreds of choices. Some of these are made unconsciously and automatically, like certain choices of word order that are dictated by the syntactic rules of language, or choices determined by the speaker's own idiosyncratic thought and language habits. Such choices cannot really be called "decisions" because the speaker is not conscious of making them. However, at least some of the choices that a speaker makes in planning any speech are consciously made and are decisions in the full sense of the word. In broadest terms message planning involves five major decision areas: (1) topic selection, (2) specific purpose formulation, (3) laying out major lines of development, (4) selecting supporting details, and (5) choice of language.

The occasions that call forth public speaking vary greatly with respect to the degree of freedom they offer the speaker to choose his topic. At one extreme are situations which give him no freedom at all. For example, an audience may invite a speaker because of his special knowledge of a certain subject, in which case they will expect him to speak on that subject and no other, or a speaker may participate in public debate on a controversial issue, in which case only speeches on that issue will be tolerated. At the other extreme are many situations that place no restrictions at all upon what the speaker may talk about. For instance, provided he gives it proper treatment, a speaker is free to talk about anything at all in most public-speaking classrooms, most entertainment situations such as after-dinner speeches, and certain purely ceremonial occasions such as commencements. Between these two extremes lie a variety of situations that offer the speaker varying degrees of choice concerning what he will talk about.

Often the speaker is restricted to a broad subject but is free within its limits to choose any specific topic on which to speak. For instance, submarine explorer Jacques-Yves Cousteau might choose to discuss quite different aspects of the broad topic of undersea exploration for different audiences. He might focus on undersea adventure, on aquatic life, submarine technology, his descents into the Mariannas Trench, the high cost of submarine exploration, safety in skin diving, or the feasibility of ocean farming. Though more or less restricted to a single broad topic, Cousteau often has considerable latitude in choosing a specific topic within the broader one. Among other factors that may contribute to the selection of the specific topic, information concerning the knowledge, attitudes, interests, and potential influence of the auditors will play a large part.

Just as knowledge about the audience may contribute to selecting a specific topic, so may it contribute to the selection of a specific purpose within the context of some long-range goal. A speaker whose ultimate goal is to build public support for a relaxation of laws concerning birth control will find many audiences so unaccustomed to the idea, so firmly opposed to it, or so ill-informed about the subject as to be unaffected or even outraged by a speech presenting direct appeals for support. Under these circumstances, the speaker may decide that his best strategy lies in adopting a more limited purpose; for example, to acquaint the audience with population statistics and predictions. For a different audience (better informed, more thoroughly acquainted with the issue, or more open-minded toward the proposed change) a speech on population statistics would at best be inefficient and at worst it might offend the audience by suggesting that the speaker had underestimated their sophistication or employed a devious approach. A specific purpose appropriate for either audience might be utterly inappropriate for the other.

The examples we have given concerning the role of audience analysis in topic selection and specific-purpose formulation have their counterparts in the finer details of message construction. As in the foregoing examples, each of these decisions (laying out major lines of development, choosing supporting details, selecting appropriate language) is involved when we become concerned with making choices among alternative ways of putting a message together. Although any given speech will not necessarily allow or require decisions in all five areas, most of the conscious choices that speakers confront in message planning fall into one of the five. In making these decisions, the speaker often must balance many factors: questions of coherence and elegance, of personal standards and taste, of economies of time and energy. Among the other considerations, factors in the audience often play a significant part.

Regardless of which message-decision area is involved, knowledge gained from audience analysis will contribute in two ways. First, information about the audience will suggest alternative courses of action; that is, considering auditors leads a speaker to think of possible topics, purposes, illustrations, and so on. Second, information about the audience will suggest choices among alternatives. For example, given two authorities to quote on wages and prices, or two ways of saying that wage increases lead to price increases, a speaker's choice between them will be influenced by the knowledge that he is addressing the CIO rather than the National Association of Manufacturers. In other words, with respect to message planning, audience analysis serves both a creative and a critical function.

**Message pretesting.** When a message is particularly important, and especially when it is to be presented many times to different audiences, it is sometimes possible to pretest it—that is, to present it to a small sample of the audience (or to a similar audience) and to observe their reactions to it. If several pretests are made, it may be possible to determine whether the message has different effects for different types of listeners or listener groups, to observe whether the predicted and desired effects of the message do in fact occur, and to note the presence of unanticipated side effects. On the basis of these findings, the message may be altered, its exposure may be limited to certain types of audiences, or it may be discarded as unsuitable.

The most widely-publicized use of message pretesting is in the preparation of commercial advertisements. A commercial is prepared that is expected to have an effect upon viewers of a certain type. It may be tailored to increase product appeal, to promote a favorable image of the advertiser, to facilitate brand loyalty, or to accomplish some other objective with a particular audience such as identity-seeking teenagers (the Pepsi Generation), status-striving suburbanites (Volkswagen) or adolescent males of all ages (Brylcreem. Are you man enough to try it?). The pretest is then run on a sample audience that usually includes some persons from the target audience and from other potential audiences as well. Responses in the various groups are recorded and compared, and auditors may be interviewed concerning such matters as their impressions of the advertiser, the product, and its competitors. Sometimes this procedure merely confirms the ad writer's prediction that the commercial would have its intended effect. However, the results of the pretest may suggest changes in the commercial or alternative ways of advertising the product or of preparing advertisements for the target audience in the future.

The message pretest has become more or less routine for nationwide advertising; however, it is also useful in any other form of communication. For instance, most self-instructional materials such as programmed textbooks and teaching machines have been pretested for effectiveness. After some unit of material (say a fifty-minute recorded lecture) has been prepared, but before it is put into widespread use, it is presented to a group of students of the age and background level for which it was intended. After exposure to the lecture, the students are tested for their retention of its content and their evaluation of its interest value and general effectiveness. If pretest results are unsatisfactory, the lecture may be revised or discarded. If they are encouraging, the instructional unit may be put into use with greater confidence and with fuller knowledge of its probable effects.

A modification of this pretesting procedure is often followed in preparing for public speaking. Proposed basic points, supporting details, turns of phrase, or even the complete speech, may be tried out on family or friends and their reactions used as a basis for retaining, modifying, or eliminating the tested material. To the student or the individual speaker who does not have access to market research agencies or educational testing services, such informal pretesting can be of material value. By selecting pretest listeners carefully and asking them the right questions, the speaker may be able to improve his effectiveness materially.

## Monitoring effects

So far we have discussed those uses of audience analysis concerned with activities and decisions taken before the message is presented to its target audience. However, audience analysis is also used during the presentation of the speech and after it is over, for the speaker may wish to know how the audience responded during the speech and what they were left with when it was finished.

Situations vary greatly with respect to the importance of knowing how the audience responded to a speech. In general, the more a speaker's course of future action will be determined by the response an audience gives to a speech, the more important it is to observe just what effect the communication has upon the audience, rather than assuming that the speech has those effects (and only those effects) that the speaker intended.

Most of us are inclined to think about the outcome of a speech in terms of whether the speaker produced the effect that he intended throughout the whole audience or in some major or important part of the audience. When listing the effects of a speech, we are likely to restrict our attention to anticipated effects only. If the speaker says that he intended to inform the audience about some object or event, we think of the effects of the speech in terms of whether the majority of the audience did in fact acquire that information. We are not likely to consider how many in the audience developed favorable or unfavorable attitudes toward the topic or the speaker, how many learned from the speech something other than what was intended, how much misinformation was read into the speech along with the facts presented, or what various auditors did with the new information after they got it.

By focusing on the audience, however, rather than on the speaker or the speech, we see quite clearly that every communication event is attended by its own particular set of consequences, and that these consequences are richly varied. Although this variety of response is present in virtually every communication situation, we may enhance our appreciation for its richness if we observe it first in some communication other than a public speech.

**Multiple effects.** Consider the case of a television commercial for a popular brand of cigarettes that portrays an attractive young couple in swim suits listening to a portable radio aboard a sailboat skimming along the shoreline against a backdrop of tree-lined beach on a sunny day. The commercial lasts sixty seconds, but during that brief interval a viewer may experience a number of effects, some of which remain with him long after the commercial has been forgotten.

As I watch the commercial, the accented rhythms of the background music may be pleasantly stimulating, and so may the behavior or the appearance of the actors. A word or phrase in the narration may strike a sympathetic note. The narrator's voice may inspire my trust, or his dialect may raise my hackles. For these and other reasons, I may attend to the commercial or largely ignore it. If I pay attention, my levels of interest and satisfaction will probably vary substantially during the sixty-second interval. At some points my blood pressure may actually increase, my pupils dilate, or my palms sweat. My eyelids may droop, or I may sit up straighter in my chair.

Watching the commercial, I may feel an urge to smoke, or make a mental note to try (or to avoid) the brand advertised, or feel better or worse disposed toward television advertising, or wonder what the world is coming to. I may recall that once I decided to take up sailing but got too busy to do it, and wonder where I can find a good used sailboat; or I may reflect that I ought to get out more often to the beach. The appearance of the actors may arouse faint guilt feelings; I may decide that now is the time for that diet, or resolve to get into the sun tomorrow, or remember that it has been a long time since I had a haircut. My desire for a transistor radio may increase. I may reinforce my image of a society filled with beautiful, affluent, fun-loving people, or be depressed by the spectacle of waste and frivolity in a world torn by unsolved problems and filled with starving millions.

From watching the commercial, I may have learned some things to look for in a cigarette (charcoal filter, light tobacco), a vocabulary for describing cigarette qualities (mildness, full-bodied flavor), a company slogan, some odds and ends about sailing, and the fact that there is a town in Rhode Island named Newport. In addition to this information, I may have changed my attitudes in subtle ways. I may be more inclined to perceive Brand X as a sophisticated ciga- rette, two-piece swim suits as interesting apparel, or sailing as a worth-while leisure-time activity. In some instances my behavior may change as well. I may start (or stop) smoking, switch to (or from) Brand X, whistle the tune to the commercial, talk more about outdoor sports, plan a picnic, or write a letter to the Federal Com- munications Commission complaining of the deteriorating taste dis- played on TV commercials. All of these things and more are possi- ble effects depending upon my experiences, prior knowledge and attitudes, and my psychological set at the time of listening.

The list of possible effects might be extended indefinitely, but even these few possibilities suggest four points worth remembering:

(1) Messages, even those we are inclined to dismiss as relatively trivial and insignificant, have effects.

(2) The same message may have different effects upon different auditors, or on the same auditor at different times.

(3) Even a short message is likely to have more than a single effect upon any given auditor.

(4) Some of the effects of a message are unlikely to have been anticipated by the message source.

**Types of effects.** Both in monitoring effects and in message pre- testing, it is important to make several distinctions among types of effects. The first of these, which is implied in the preceding ex- ample, is a distinction between dominant and idiosyncratic message effects. In one sense, of course, all message effects are idiosyncratic because all message effects occur within individuals; however, some effects are much more likely to occur among individuals in a given audience than are others. An effect that we have reason to believe will occur or that we have observed to occur among a significant fraction of a given audience may be called a **dominant effect.** This terminology does not imply that dominant effects control the behav- ior of the individual auditor to a greater extent than other effects, but simply that, when we look at the responses of all of the audi- tors, the dominant effects occur very frequently.

An effect that we have reason to believe will occur or that we have observed to occur among only a few auditors may be called an

**idiosyncratic effect.** For many auditors the strongest effect of the speech will be the idiosyncratic effects that the message has upon them. Generally we use the dominant reactions of an audience to generalize about how the audience as a whole responded to the speech, but these dominant responses usually leave out of consideration a wealth of qualitatively different individual responses.

A second important distinction among message effects, also suggested by the TV commercial example, is a distinction between anticipated effects and surprise effects. An **anticipated effect** is either one that the speaker deliberately set out to achieve or it is a side-effect that he recognized probably would occur and that he was prepared to accept. Of course, an anticipated effect may not occur in any sizeable fraction of an audience, but if the speaker is looking for it, then either its occurrence or its nonoccurrence will be noted. One of the purposes of audience analysis is to eliminate **surprise effects,** so if audience analysis has been effective, then most surprise effects will be idiosyncratic. When a dominant effect is unanticipated, the surprise may be a happy one or it may be disastrous.

A third and final distinction among message effects is the distinction between process and product effects. A **process effect** is one that occurs during the speech and is subject to modification by subsequent portions of the message; it is what goes on in the listener as he listens to the speech. A **product effect** is one that is left as a residue after the message has concluded. I may or may not thrill to the language of a brilliant orator (process), but whether I do or not, I may remember his words and quote them later (product).

Strictly speaking, of course, this distinction between process and product is invalid because every response of an audience is an effect of whatever stimuli produced it, and there are no "process effects" but only "processes." Effect follows effect in the speech until the speaker stops talking, and what have here been called "product effects" are simply the difference between the listener's states at the beginning and at the end of the speech. On the other hand, to talk conveniently about the effects of speeches, which are really not single stimuli but are complicated sequences of stimuli, we need some verbal shorthand for distinguishing between what happens from moment to moment during the speech, on the one hand, and what change has been produced by the whole sequence, on the other; and we shall therefore find it convenient to distinguish as we have here between process and product effects.

In discussing certain types of public speaking, we often devote all of our attention to product effects—to "what comes of the speech" —and tend to overlook process effects—the brief, subtle changes in the auditor from moment to moment during the speech. But process effects are of great interest in communication for two reasons.

First, it is through process effects that product effects come about. If a listener is somehow different after the speech than he was beforehand, it is extremely unlikely that he changed all at once at some critical point in the speech. On the contrary, he was probably led to his new position through a series of minute steps, each almost imperceptible yet each contributing to their combined effect.

Second, communication often is presented and received largely for the sake of the process effects themselves, though our customary way of talking about communication tends to prevent us from recognizing this fact. When a person has seen a good play or heard a powerful eulogy, or watched an exciting TV drama, or laughed at a fine after-dinner speech, he is likely to say that he has been entertained or moved or inspired or amused. But the primary objective of such communications as these is not to produce some terminal state of entertainment or emotion after the message is over; it is to evoke a changing pattern of reaction and response while the communication is in process, while it is still going on. To be sure, we may be "left with a message" or feel "transformed" afterward, but the participation in such communication events is rewarding even when we do not feel much differently afterward than we did beforehand, for the primary value of such messages is realized during, not after, their presentation.

We need to remember that the effects of communication are important to the communicator for three main reasons. First, as implied earlier in discussing communication strategy, the speaker's purpose in speaking is generally phrased in terms of the effects that he hopes to produce in the audience, so that settling upon a purpose involves specifying desired effects. Second, it is with an eye to effects that other elements in the communication strategy are most often evaluated and chosen. Finally, when the consequences of a given message will be used as a basis for deciding future plans, some method of detecting relevant effects is essential.

## Two modes of audience analysis

In the foregoing discussion of the role of audience analysis in communication strategy we have not touched upon either of two important questions: (1) What is it useful to know about an audience? (2) How do you use the information once it is in hand? In one sense, most of the remainder of this book is devoted to answering these questions, but in another sense, both questions are unanswerable. Before going further it is essential to understand what sort of answers can be given to these two vital questions and to understand the extent to which it is impossible to provide complete answers, for it is only through such an understanding that we can avoid being misled by our own efforts to think systematically about the analysis of audiences. We can approach this understanding most conveniently by contrasting two forms of audience analysis: demographic and purpose-oriented.

**Demographic analysis.** The first mode of audience analysis was proposed by the ancient Greek philosopher-scientist Aristotle. He advised the speaker to consider such characteristics of his audience as age and wealth, because these tend to make an individual more susceptible to some arguments and ideas and less responsive to others. He even sketched out a sort of crude audience typology· Old Men are prone to be deliberate, are less moved by passions, are cautious, and the like; Young Men are self-confident, venturesome, inclined to action more than words, and so forth.

The general properties of a group, such as age, sex, income, place of residence, occupation, marital status, size of household, political party preference, years of schooling, religion, and other such characteristics are called its **demographic characteristics.** An audience analysis based upon them may be called a **demographic audience analysis.** It is this approach to audience analysis that first comes to mind, to begin by recording certain standard information about an audience and then, on the basis of experience and research, to infer about the audience such matters as knowledge, temperament, attitudes, habits of thought, language preferences, or other matters that will enter into their responses to communication. The demographic characteristics are **observed;** they are then used as a basis for **inferences** concerning matters related to the speaker, speech, and occasion.

When demographic information about the audience is available, it almost invariably proves valuable to the speaker to examine it and reflect upon it. The phrase "reflect upon it" is deliberately chosen in this instance, for it suggests a ruminative, creative, relatively unsystematic sort of mental activity rather than a rigorous application of principle. The demographic information about an audience often will **suggest** specific content, treatment, or approach, but there is no standard formula for extracting speech ideas from demographic audience analysis. A moment's reflection will show why this is so.

To begin with, there is no way of knowing what demographic characteristics will be most useful in a given case because **any** property of the audience might be useful in some cases, but **no** property of the audience is invariably useful. For example, in discussing water fluoridation a speaker would find it helpful to know how many Christian Scientists are in the audience, although ordinarily the knowledge that he is addressing a group composed mostly of Christian Scientists would at most suggest an example or a comparison but certainly have a very small effect, if any, on the speech. On political topics it is important to know how many members of the John Birch Society or Americans for Democratic Action are in the audience, but on nonpolitical topics this information usually will be of very limited use.

Consequently, though persuaders and rhetoricians throughout history have wished for an ideal list of audience characteristics that could be used as a basis for audience analysis in every situation, all efforts to find such a list have ended in frustration. People and communication are too variable.

This is not to say that a given speaker might not devise a list of audience characteristics important to his own particular communication problems. On the contrary, because a given speaker is likely to operate within a relatively limited range with respect to purpose, audience, topic, and occasion, such a list of important audience characteristics might be extremely useful to him. But such a list must grow out of his own experience and include only those questions about audience characteristics that he has found important for his purposes. The same list would be of far less value to another speaker.

**Purpose-oriented analysis.** A second mode of audience analysis begins from an entirely different point of view. Instead of initiating the analysis by asking some standard set of questions about audience characteristics, this approach begins by asking what about the audience is most likely to be important in light of the speaker's purposes. The search for information about the audience is then governed by what it is that the speaker needs to know about his audience in the context of a given communication situation.

To see how the purpose-oriented approach might work in a specific case, let us suppose that you are to make a speech on the structure of the United Nations, the major purpose of which is to improve your audience's grasp of how that organization works. If you were following a purpose-oriented approach, you would begin the analysis by asking yourself just what you needed to know about the audience in order to enhance their knowledge of the UN as far as possible. Some of your information requirements would be clear at the outset; however, in order to determine your needs fully, you would have to work out a preliminary plan for the speech. This preliminary speech plan would tell you about additional information that you might like to have, and on the basis of that additional information the preliminary plan might be revised. It is even possible that this revised speech plan might suggest needs for still further information about the audience, which might lead to still further revisions in the speech plan. Working back and forth between speech plan and audience analysis, your speech would gradually take on the shape which was, in your judgment, best suited to accomplish your purpose with the particular audience. The following considerations are a sample of the issues you might confront.

To begin with, you would want to know how much information your audience already had about the UN. Without this information you might very well waste your entire effort by "informing" your audience mostly about things they already knew or by assuming that they had background for your speech which in fact they did not have. In either case you would add little to their knowledge.

We may pause for a moment to consider how you might get such information. In very rare cases, you might be able to pre-test a representative sample of the audience in order to determine how much they know about the UN but ordinarily you would at best be able to talk informally with one or two representative audience members. By establishing their general level of knowledge and asking them questions about other audience members they know, you may be able to get a fair idea of the average level of audience knowledge about the topic. This approach will be especially useful if the audience is composed of members of a well-defined group such as a civic club, professional or business organization, fraternal or other society with regular meetings and frequent interpersonal contact, for the members of such natural groups have much in common and often know a good deal about one another.

At worst, you may have to try to infer knowledge of the UN from general audience characteristics. Based on your own previous experiences with the topic, you may have some idea concerning how much the average listener knows about the UN; you may then ask whether this audience has any special characteristics that would cause it to know less or more about the topic than the average audience. For instance, if they were a high school group, you might want to check whether they had recently studied the UN. If they were predominantly over fifty and without more than average education for persons of that age, you might infer that they would know relatively little about the structure of the organization, although they might have general information about its more publicized activities.

With a general picture of audience knowledge in mind, you could now begin to plan a speech designed to build upon what they already knew. As you added each new thread to the fabric of your message, you would test it against your knowledge of, or inferences about, the audience. For instance, suppose you consider the possibility of illustrating the UN's lack of sovereignty by comparing it with the American confederation of pre-Constitutional times. As American citizens, your audience will almost certainly know of the confederation, but how much about it will they know? In order for the comparison to be really effective, will you have to tell them as much about the confederation as you would have to tell them about the UN to make the same point? With some auditors, such as college sophomores who have been exposed recently to American history, the comparison might work rather well; but for other auditors, such as middle-aged members of an Indiana Grange, the comparison would probably take more explaining than it would be worth.

The judgment of what it is worth, of course, has to be made within the context of a speaker's particular purpose(s). The limited value of the confederation comparison in this case extends only to its information value. As you reflect upon the example, it may seem very appropriate to you in the context of your total purpose, and you may feel strongly disposed to use it even though it adds no information. If this happens, you may pause a moment to consider whether information really is your only purpose. Is it possible that in the back of your mind, all along, you have been hoping to show your audience that the UN is a workable idea that deserves our increased support and needs more power to operate effectively? If so, then the confederation example is entirely appropriate whether it informs or not, for it will serve to associate the UN (something your audience may feel uneasy or mildly distrustful about) with the growth of the American government. Whether they recall, or have ever been exposed to, the full details of the post-Revolutionary era, they certainly will have been told at some time about the difficulties experienced by the confederation and will have learned to regard the Constitutional Convention as necessary and desirable. The comparison of the confederation with the UN will then tend to establish in their minds an image of the world organization that is consistent with your subsidiary purpose.

With this secondary purpose in mind, it becomes important to accumulate some additional information about the audience: Do they display any special characteristics that might predispose them for or against the UN? Many people who were of literate age during the early years of the League of Nations, for instance, will tend to associate the UN with the League, which failed in its purpose to preserve world peace. How many of your auditors fall into that age group? Would it be better to ignore the League altogether, hoping that your audience will do so too, or would it be better to compare the League with the UN to show the differences between them? Is your subsidiary purpose important enough to warrant your spending much preparation or speaking time on such a comparison? Or, having thought of the comparison originally as a persuasive device, can you use it, nevertheless, for informational purposes? Would such a comparison add a dimension of understanding to the speech for auditors of the type to whom you will speak? And if so, is it possible, in light of their special characteristics, to combine the informational and the persuasive purpose in the single comparison so as to contribute toward both effects with a single unit of content?

We have only sampled here some of the kinds of issues that arise during the course of purpose-oriented audience analysis. To begin with, we have observed that this form of audience analysis is not limited to a single information-gathering stage before the speech is planned. On the contrary, this form of audience analysis continues throughout the entire message preparation. Second, we have observed that the information about the audience is not gathered according to some predetermined formula but is determined by the needs of the speaker as he makes decisions concerning the content and desired effects of his message. Third, we have noted that there is a complex set of relations among audience, purpose, and content: (1) It is not possible to know in advance just what or how much information about the audience will be required in a given case. (2) Special characteristics of an audience may suggest including or excluding certain content. (3) During the analysis the speaker may discover previously hidden purposes of his own. (4) The newly-revealed purposes may lead to needs for additional knowledge about the audience. All of these must be worked out through various stages of development and may lead the speaker in somewhat unpredictable directions.

Audience analysis which is purpose-oriented, then, is not a stage of speech preparation; it is a dynamic and integral part of every stage of speech preparation.

**Technology and art in audience analysis.** Having contrasted the two dominant modes of audience analysis, we now are in a position to consider what sort of answers may be given to the two questions: (1) What is it useful to know about an audience? (2) How do you use the information once it is in hand? We must interpret these questions in light of the fact that in most instances audience analysis is not so much a technology as it is an art.

In a well-developed technology, such as automotive engineering, bridge design, steelmaking, or electronics, decision rules covering most of the relevant possibilities are already worked out or may be constructed from comprehensive theories. Establishing rules is possible because the number of factors that must be taken into account is predictable and the range of possible desirable outcomes is relatively restricted.

In the case of an art, however, the exact factors that must be taken into account in solving a particular problem are unpredictable, and the range of desired outcomes is either infinite or else so large as to be virtually so. Under these circumstances, decision rules may be formulated to cover a few recurring problems, but most problems must be approached individually. In music, psychiatry, teaching, and architecture, for example, practice may be influenced by general principles but cannot be dictated by decision rules.

As we noted earlier, something like a limited technology of audience analysis is possible for a single speaker operating in a limited range of communication situations and pursuing a limited set of goals. Under these circumstances the possibilities are sufficiently reduced in number that the communicator may hope eventually to formulate decision rules covering most or all of them. But in the general case no such analysis is possible. Ignoring speaker and media for a moment, the communication formula provides us with three other factors—the topic, the context, and the desired effects that must be taken into account in determining what we may need to know about a particular audience. For each combination of a certain type of topic, context, and effect, we should require a particular type of information about the audience. Given no more than one hundred varieties of topic, context, and effect, we would have one million combinations of the three to be taken into account in specifying the type of audience information required. If we now add considerations of speaker and media, this number is multiplied many times over, and the number of different patterns of demand for audience information reaches into the billions.

To understand how it is possible to operate in a universe of so many possibilities, we need to appreciate the difference between two kinds of decision principles: the algorithmic and the hueristic. The difference between them can be illustrated by comparing the way we learn to play chess and tic-tac-toe. It is possible to formulate a set of decision rules for tic-tac-toe that are essentially infallible; they guarantee the player who uses them that he will at worst play to a draw and that he will never lose. The rules specify all of the possible situations in the game and provide a rule to follow in every situation. Chess, on the other hand, cannot be played in this fashion; to be sure, it is possible to formulate rules that work most of the time, but a good chess player can always win against an opponent who is following a rigid system of rules. The number of possible positions on the chess board is so vast that there is no single move that is always best. Good chess players operate with certain very general principles in mind, several of which may apply to the decision concerning a single move. The player uses these general principles as a basis for analyzing any given board situation, but his specific decision is governed by the particular situation in which he finds himself. The principles of tic-tac-toe are algorithmic; the principles of chess are hueristic. Chess principles give the player some help in analyzing the situation, but they do not lead him through to a foregone conclusion in the same way that the tic-tac-toe principles do.

When we say that audience analysis principles are hueristic, we do not mean that they are vague or indefinite but only that they must be used in a certain way. They must be understood as a means of getting into the analysis, as tools for thinking about the audience situation, as suggestive principles only. If we try to develop algorithms for audience analysis—rules that are capable of carrying us rigorously through a complete analysis to communication decisions —or if we try to treat whatever principles are developed as if they could be made to work in this way, then valid and effective analysis will always be beyond our reach. It is only when we understand audience analytic techniques as beginning points for analysis that we can use them effectively.

What this means is that the communicator must, at some point in his analysis of the audience, formulate his own analytic principles to cover the specific situation in which he finds himself. General principles may get him started and set the direction of his analysis, but when he gets into the details of the problem, he will usually find himself on his own without specific recommendations to follow and with only general principles to guide him.

At this point education and experience become especially important in communication. One reason why educated and experienced individuals almost invariably communicate more effectively than uneducated and inexperienced ones is that they know more about people, and consequently they are able to determine more readily than others just what it would be useful to know about their auditors and how to interpret the information once they have it. If I do not know that most Southern Baptists are opposed to dancing for religious reasons, then I will not be alert to the presence of Baptists in making my speech on recreational opportunities in the campus area; and even if I should by accident come across the fact that there were Baptists in my audience, I would not know how to put this information to use.

That is why neither this book nor any other treatment of audience analysis can substitute for education and experience in analyzing audiences and formulating strategies of communication. Anything at all about an auditor may be useful on some occasion for predicting how he will respond to communication, regardless of whether we are using a demographic or a purpose-oriented mode of analysis, and the more a speaker knows about people and their society, the greater will be the variety of different ways in which he may understand and respond to his auditors.

But hueristic principles may get an analysis started, and our purpose here will be to suggest beginning points and general frameworks for audience analysis in a variety of communication situations. They will be useful to the communicator in proportion to his knowledge and experience; the more he knows and has experienced, the more these suggestive principles will suggest to him.

# FOUR

# Measurement and inference

Once a communicator has decided what information he needs about his auditors he faces the task of obtaining it. Some of the information he requires will be available to him through direct observation of one kind or another, but other information that he needs will not be directly available to him and must be inferred from whatever information is available. Moreover, if he has accumulated information about individual auditors, he confronts the task of combining this information in such a way as to make valid generalizations about the audience.

This chapter will be concerned with general questions of measurement and inference as these apply to the analysis of audience characteristics and response. We shall be concerned with what is meant by "measurement," with the instruments and techniques by which observations are made, with the extent to which important characteristics are observable as opposed to the degree to which they must be inferred, and with some problems involved in generalizing about the audience on the basis of measurements made upon auditors.

## What is measurement?

The term "measurement" is used in several different ways, two of which must be distinguished in discussing the problem of measuring audience predispositions and responses. When we say, "The room measures 32 feet long," and when we say, "His IQ measures 105," we appear to be making similar statements in both cases. Both statements imply that we have some standard or yardstick that is appropriate to whatever is being measured and that may be applied in one case to rooms and in the other case to IQ's. The fact is, however, that these two senses of the verb "to measure" are really quite different, and it is essential to appreciate this difference in order to understand the role of data about auditors in predicting response to communication.

When we apply a tape measure or a yardstick to a table or a room in order to measure its length, our concern is with a characteristic that the room or table and the yardstick have in common. The length of an object is a characteristic of it that is directly observable to our senses, and it is that directly observable characteristic of the object that the yardstick measures. A yardstick "measures," then, in the sense that it quantifies an observable characteristic.

However, an IQ test does no such thing. To be sure, "intelligence" is a term with many definitions, but none of those definitions suggests a directly observable characteristic of the individual. Whether it is "reasoning power" or "learning ability" or "information processing capacity" or "problem-solving ability," intelligence cannot be observed with any of the senses; moreover, though all of the aforementioned qualities may be thought of as characteristic of people, none of them is ever thought of as a characteristic of an intelligence test. An intelligence test presents the examinee with a series of particular questions to answer and problems to solve. It is the proportion of questions answered and problems solved "correctly" that determines the IQ score.

In this case, unlike the yardstick, we are not interested primarily in what we can observe of the examinee's performance. The fact that he can or cannot answer certain questions or solve certain problems is in itself a pretty trivial matter. We are interested in his answers to the IQ test items because we believe that those answers enable us to **infer** a certain level of general mental ability. The measurement of the length of a table rests upon observation only; the measurement of the IQ of a person rests upon observation plus inference.

## Observation vs. inference of auditor traits and responses

Many of the characteristics that speakers feel it important to know about auditors are not directly observable but must be inferred from things that can be observed. We will find it instructive to examine briefly what kinds of auditor information speakers most often find useful and to inquire to what extent this information is directly accessible to observation.

**Predisposing characteristics.** In the first stages of preparation for communication, speakers are usually most interested in those characteristics of the auditor that might be called "predisposing characteristics." The speaker realizes that the elements of his message will not lead to a predetermined or automatic response that is uniform for all auditors; he understands that whatever effect the message has will be mediated through the characteristics of his individual auditors, and he is interested in knowing about characteristics of the auditors that will predispose them to respond one way or another to alternate forms of the message.

Specifically, the speaker will be interested in the auditor's interest and information about the topic of his message and about other topics that may be relevant to his discussion of it; he will be interested in the attitudes and opinions that the auditor has formed about the topic and about related topics; and he will be interested in the auditor's memories, images, and associations surrounding the topic of the message and surrounding related topics. These are the characteristics of the auditor that we are inclined to believe will predispose him to respond one way or another during the speech.

It is interesting to note that not a single one of these characteristics of the auditor is directly observable. Because each of us is used to describing his own behavior and experience in terms of what appear to us to be very real interests, knowledge, attitudes, opinions, memories, images and associations, we tend to attribute the behavior of others to similar causes, and we believe that we can see these internal states of others reflected in their overt behavior. But the key word here is "reflected"; we do not see the predisposing characteristics themselves, for they are internal states of the individual. Instead, we see "reflections" of the states or characteristics, which permit us to infer their presence. When we say, "He is interested in firearms," or "She knows a good deal about real estate," or "He has a negative attitude toward the city government," or "She puts Freud in the same class with Einstein," we are not making observations of the people in question but are making, instead, inferences based on our observations of their behavior.

Thus, the speaker can have no direct knowledge about the internal states of his auditors but must rely on inference for whatever information of this kind he gets. He may base such inferences on the auditor's verbal behavior, his history of previous experience, his demographic characteristics, or his group memberships.

If the speaker can obtain reliable knowledge about it, an auditor's history of previous experience may yield a wealth of useful inferences about his present internal states and probable response tendencies. A college student who has participated in a protest march is likely to differ in certain ways from a student who has never done so; the protest marcher's view of society and his image of himself and of the way he fits into society are likely to differ to some extent from the corresponding views of the nonprotestor. If he has participated in more than one such demonstration, it is quite likely that he will have come to share certain characteristic beliefs and attitudes with other demonstrators. This combination of outlook, beliefs, and attitudes will affect the way he responds to certain kinds of communication. It will bias his interests, govern his interpretation of many messages, and predispose him to accept some statements and reject others.

In short, from the observed fact of participation in protest demonstrations, we may infer certain internal states. Of course, for any given individual, these inferences may be entirely wrong. A given student might engage in this form of activity for any one of dozens of possible reasons, only some of which would warrant inferences about his political and social views. But statistically speaking, the inference is probably warranted; that is, in an audience containing a high proportion of auditors with a history of social protest demonstration it is reasonably certain that the "political protest" point of view will represent a dominant source of audience response.

Similar statements could be made about people who have taken a course in public speaking, people who have lived in house trailers, men who have been under fire in combat, people who have had a major operation, people who have traveled abroad, people who have been in business for themselves, and so on. If the speaker understands these experiences himself, then he can make inferences about knowledge, beliefs, associations, and other internal conditions of an auditor who has undergone the experiences. To be sure, his inferences have only a probabilistic value. For a given auditor they are not certain to be valid, but for an audience containing many auditors with the experience in question, the inference is quite likely to characterize a dominant factor of auditor response.

The problem of measurement in this instance is that of establishing the proportion of auditors in a given audience who have had the experience in question. The fact of the experience is used as a basis for inferring nonobservable characteristics of the auditor, and these in turn are used as a basis for predicting probable response to communication.

The primary value of demographic characteristics as a basis for predicting audience response to communication is that they generally serve to distinguish groups of people who have had certain experiences in common and therefore have come to share ideas, perceptions, values and especially, as we shall see in the next chapter, images in common.

Again, however, demographic characteristics are of interest to the speaker only because they serve as a basis for inferring the auditor's internal states. Although it is by no means certain, an individual who is a parent is more likely to have particular attitudes and beliefs and certain bits of information concerning the home and children than is another individual who is not a parent, and in a group containing a high proportion of parents, these attitudes and beliefs and this knowledge may be taken as a fairly reliable basis for predicting response to communication.

Again, the measurement problem is that of determining the proportion of auditors who have a particular demographic characteristic: how many are farmers, or Unitarians, or Italian immigrants, or earn between $7,000 and $10,000 per year, or owe on a mortgage, or are over 40 years of age, or have whatever other characteristic the speaker believes to be important to predicting probable response to a given communication. The demographic characteristics can be used as a basis for prediction because they tend to be accompanied by certain ideas and feelings that lead to a predisposition to respond in a characteristic way to certain stimuli.

Of all demographic characteristics, membership in well-defined, face-to-face groups should be singled out as a matter of special significance in audience analysis. Although there are perhaps a few ideas, images, and beliefs that are shared by all Methodists, these universal traits are probably very few in number and operate rarely in communication. On the other hand, there are many more ideas and beliefs that are shared among the members of a particular Methodist congregation; these commonly-held ideas are continuously reinforced by day-to-day contact, and probably operate to shape much of the individual parishioner's response to communication.

In general, as we have observed elsewhere, membership in groups that meet often face to face serves to make group members more alike in many ways. Certainly internal states such as attitudes and beliefs are among the most important ways in which members of face-to-face groups grow alike through repeated interaction and exposure to the same stimuli. It is these attitudes and beliefs and other internal states of the auditor that serve as warrants for predicting audience response, rather than membership in the group as such.

Although experiences, demographic characteristics, and group memberships provide sometimes excellent grounds for inferring nonobservable or "internal" predisposing states of auditors, perhaps the most widely used and highly valued basis for such inferences is the auditor's verbal behavior. It is useful to the speaker regardless of whether it is elicited by systematic questions or is taken as it occurs spontaneously. The two types of verbal behavior obtained under these differing conditions give somewhat different kinds of information about the auditor, and we shall reserve for later a discussion of verbal behavior obtained by systematic questioning.

Spontaneous verbal behavior, thoughtfully analyzed, can give information about the auditor's knowledge, attitudes, and interests. A thorough discussion of the methods for analyzing and interpreting verbal behavior (these methods are called "content analysis") would be out of place here, nor is it really necessary for our present purposes. For the most part, content analysis represents a sophisticated way of extracting from a message information that a sensitive reader or listener could probably get from a careful reading of the message, particularly if the message were short. The difference is that content analysis makes its estimates quantitatively and enables the observer to work with many messages or with long ones.

To begin with, the amount of content on a given topic is significant. In general, if an individual talks or writes a great deal about one subject and less about another, and if we can find nothing in the context to account for the difference, then we are justified in inferring that the first topic is more salient for him or, in more common terms, that he is more interested in it. A man who talks a lot about hounds is probably interested in hounds.

Moreover, the relative amounts of content devoted to different subtopics while discussing some larger topic gives an indication of the relative importance of the various subtopics in the individual's thinking about the larger topic. For instance, if, of the total time I spend talking about automobiles, I spend a great proportion of it talking about appearance, then you are justified in making a preliminary inference that styling is, for me, a relatively important or salient feature of automobiles.

Knowledge, too, is reflected in one's verbal behavior. If I talk a long time about the problems of public education, and never mention the Conant report, then it is a fair inference that I do not know about it. On the other hand, if I cite some of its findings accurately and in detail, then you will be led to infer that I have an intimate knowledge of it; that is, you can be certain that I know what I have repeated, and you will infer that I know more about it than I have said. To be sure, I may have deliberately misled you by citing a few facts in detail, anticipating that you would infer broader knowledge than I actually have. But the fact that this strategy may be used occasionally to deceive rests upon the fact that ordinarily, when a person displays detailed and accurate knowledge about some aspects of a topic, he also has detailed and accurate knowledge about other aspects of it. If the generalization were not usually true, it could not be used as a basis for deception. Thus, in the absence of a known intent to mislead, an auditor whose verbal output reflects some detailed knowledge of a topic may be inferred to have other knowledge that he has not displayed.

Beliefs and attitudes are also reflected in verbal behavior. If you are opposed to federal aid to higher education, it will be extremely difficult for you to talk about the topic without revealing your bias, and, unless you are making a conscious effort to conceal your opinion, it will be obvious almost from the first word you utter on the topic. Not only will it be clear whether you favor or oppose the idea, but the intensity of your feelings also will be apparent from a sufficiently large sample of your talk about it. It is one thing to say, "Farm price supports are ineffective," and something else again to say, "Farm price supports are the most diabolical scheme ever conceived for extending bureaucratic control over the farmer." Both statements oppose farm price supports, but the latter is a much more intense expression of disapproval.

As we have seen, the predisposing characteristics of auditors that are of greatest general interest to speakers are such internal states as attitudes, beliefs, knowledge, images, and associations. The speaker is interested in these characteristics because they enable him to make certain predictions of audience response; yet none of these characteristics is observable. They may be inferred from the auditor's known experience, his demographic characteristics, his group memberships, and especially from his verbal behavior. The inferences in each case have a probabilistic value. For a given single auditor they may or may not be true; for moderately large audiences containing a high proportion of auditors with similar experiences, group memberships, demographic characteristics, or patterns of verbal behavior, these observables provide a fairly reliable basis for inferring internal states of auditors that will serve as substantial factors in determining audience response to communication.

**Process responses.** Speakers often want to know how their auditors are responding from moment to moment during the speech. In an earlier chapter we referred to these momentary reactions as process responses, and three are of special interest: (1) attention (or interest), (2) comprehension (or understanding), and (3) evaluation (or approval and acceptance).

As in the case of predisposing characteristics, these process responses are all internal states of the listener. None of them is directly observable, though we are inclined to believe that we can infer attention, comprehension, and evaluation from observable signs. In general, these signs fall into three categories: physiological processes as measured by electronic devices, the auditor's continuous recordings of subjective responses as obtained by audience analyzers devices, and the auditor's observable behavior during the speech.

Of the three observable bases for inferring audience process responses, physiological measurements have been applied less often and less systematically than the other two, although they show some promise of developing into useful approaches to audience measurement. In the next section of this chapter, we shall mention some specific physiological measurements that might be applied to audience analysis, but for the moment it is sufficient to note that many subjective states are accompanied by physiological changes that may be measured by devices attached to the surface of the skin. The physiological processes are thought to yield useful information about the auditor's subjective states.

The lie detector is based on just this principle. Physiological measuring devices are attached to the person being questioned, and the records of his physiological processes are compared with his answers to questions. If, during the period of his answer to a particular question, the physiological processes show remarkable change, that answer is regarded as questionable. Much additional information about the person's background and the details of the question must be brought to bear in determining whether a given answer is probably truthful or not, but the interpretation rests upon the generalization that one cannot tell a lie without experiencing some degree of physiological arousal.

Of course, the lie detector does not always work as expected. Apparently there are some individuals who can lie without experiencing any physical change, though such persons are truly rare. On the other hand, there are many people who experience arousal under any kind of questioning regardless of the truthfulness of their answers, and others who feel a sense of guilt sufficient to produce arousal even when they are in fact innocent. The records of these individuals "reflect" guilt and lying even when there is no objective basis for it.

The problems of interpreting the results of the lie detector tests are indicative of the general problems involved in interpreting physiological data as responses to particular stimuli. We can be reasonably confident that a physical change represents a response to some stimulus, but it is often very difficult to determine just what the stimulus was that produced the response. This problem is particularly severe when we deal with response to continuous sequences of stimuli such as extended verbal messages. Does profound arousal at a given point in the speech indicate a response to something that is being said at that time, or to something that the speaker said earlier and about which the listener is still thinking, or to some extraneous thought that is completely unrelated to the speech?

A second major problem involved in interpreting physiological response data is that of determining just what subjective state is associated with the physiological response. Although a little progress has been made toward interpreting the relation of various patterns of physical response with the different "emotions," in general the most we can say with assurance at this time is that physiological arousal means that the subject is experiencing **some** emotional state. In order to describe the state, we need additional information.

If we present our subject with a large, hairy spider in a jar and observe a profound physiological change, we are probably justified in inferring that the change does not reflect pleasure or desire on the subject's part. But ordinarily in a speech the stimulus is not sufficiently universal in its implications to warrant strong inferences about the subjective state associated with a particular physiological response. In these cases, we ordinarily must obtain supplemental information by asking the auditor what he was experiencing at a particular point.

The physiological response tells us that something was happening at a particular point in the speech and may serve as a rough index of the intensity of the auditor's reaction; but the nature of the response is, for the most part, difficult to infer from the physical data alone. To be sure, if the level of arousal is moderately high, we may infer that the auditor is paying attention to some feature of the message (though we may not be sure just what feature of it is serving as his focus of attention). And conversely, if the arousal level is very low, we may infer that the subject is going to sleep. Thus, physiological measurements may provide some basis for inferring level of attention to the message. However, they can tell us nothing about the subject's level of understanding during the speech, and they require supplementary data in order to tell us much about the emotional impact of the message on the auditor.

Much more commonly used than physiological response data is the data obtained from devices called "audience analyzers." The audience analyzer or, as it is called in television research, the program analyzer, is a device on which the auditor records voluntarily and continuously some aspect of his reaction to a message while he is receiving it. He may record how "interesting" he finds the message from moment to moment, or to what extent he "agrees" with what is being said, or whether he finds it "clear," or any other single aspect of his moment-to-moment response to the message.

Our inference concerning the implications of audience analyzer responses rests upon the assumption that the auditor is able to tell the truth about what he is experiencing, and that he is willing to do so. In effect, although the analyzer results appear in the form of numerical data, we are basing our inference upon essentially verbal responses of the subject. That is, he is substituting analyzer responses for words in telling us that he found some portions of the speech very clear, other portions fairly clear, still other portions very unclear, and so on. And therefore these data are open to exactly the same reservations that we apply to any report from an individual concerning what he experienced, felt, or thought at a given time.

The principal advantage of the audience analyzer results is that the subject is spared any lapses of memory by making his record of response continuously as he listens. However, he may not know exactly how he is responding; he may become engrossed in the message; or he may be utterly bored with it and forget to record any changes of reaction. He may deliberately falsify his reactions in order to appear agreeable or to conform to some idea of how he ought to react under given circumstances. If he is unable to respond truthfully or unwilling to do so, then the audience analyzer results will not reflect his internal or subjective states during the speech. But if he is willing and able to report accurately, then the data may be used to infer attention, comprehension, evaluation, or any other conscious process response.

More often than any other type of information, the overt behavior of the audience is used as a basis for inferring process responses to communication. The speaker who maintains close visual directness with his audience is constantly monitoring their behavior and on that basis inferring their momentary responses to his speech. Motion pictures are sometimes made of audiences watching a movie or a play or listening to a speech, and their posture, movements, facial expressions, and the like used to infer whether they are paying attention, are interested, find the message agreeable, or understand what is being said.

The basis for such inferences is the assumption that there exist (at least within our culture) fairly uniform connections between internal states and certain behavioral manifestations. For example, we assume that one's attention is focused upon what his eyes are looking toward. An auditor who is sitting straight in his chair, looking at the speaker, is thought to be more interested and attentive than one who is leaning back in his seat with his eyes closed. An auditor who scowls and draws his lips into a thin line is thought to be angry. One who shakes his head disagrees or fails to understand. An auditor who fidgets about in his seat is less interested than one who sits still. The list of such inferences could be extended, but the point is that inferences drawn from overt behavior rest upon the assumption of conventional and fairly uniform associations between internal states and overt behaviors.

Sometimes these inferences prove to be wrong. The auditor may have closed his eyes in order to concentrate more fully on the flow of ideas. He may be scowling out of an effort to connect what the speaker is saying with some recent experience. He may fidget out of excitement about what the speaker is saying. In short, the behavioral manifestations are not invariably and uniformly associated with internal conditions. But the very fact that we do watch our auditors for signs of response reflects the statistical validity of our inferences. Though they are not infallible, they are so generally correct that every normal speaker in our culture has learned to look for these signs in his auditors and adjusts his language behavior accordingly. (At least, that is what is normally done in conversational situations; the public speaker who may have a rigidly-planned speech prepared and who is unprepared to deviate from it may deliberately choose not to look for signs of auditor response.)

It is the statistical validity of inferences based on observations of audience behavior that makes such observations useful in audience analysis. In the absence of any ability to observe directly an auditor's attention, comprehension, and evaluation during the course of a speech, his overt behavior supplies the most readily available empirical basis for inferring them.

The process responses with which speakers are most concerned are attention, comprehension, and evaluation, but, as we have seen, all of these responses are nonobservable. They are inferred from physiological response, audience analyzer recordings, and overt behavior.

Inferences in all three cases are subject to error. It is difficult to attribute physiological responses to particular features of the speech and also difficult to interpret their relation to the subjective states that are of interest. Audience analyzer recordings are valid only to the extent that the auditor is willing and able to report his reactions accurately. Behavioral manifestations may in a given instance have different causes than a conventional interpretation of the auditor behavior might suggest.

Nevertheless, these observable responses yield the best available estimates of the auditor's corresponding internal or subjective response. Although their interpretation may or may not be true for a given auditor, for a sizable audience displaying very similar observable reactions they may be interpreted with somewhat greater confidence.

**Product responses.** After a speech is over, the speaker may wish to know what effect it had upon the auditors. In general, he will be interested in three classes of response to the speech-as-a-whole. These three classes of "product response," as we have previously labeled them, are the auditor's internal state, his overt behavior, and his verbal behavior.

The stated principal objective of many speeches is to affect some particular internal state of the auditor: to cause him to think about a topic, to lead him to see a question in some new light, to give him information, or to change his opinion or his attitude. All of these goals have reference to internal, nonobservable states in the auditor. In general, they will be inferred from verbal behavior in much the same way as we outlined in discussing verbal behavior as an index to predisposing characteristics earlier in this chapter, and we need not discuss them further here.

Sometimes, however, the actual goal of a speech is to affect the verbal behavior of the auditor in its own right. That is, sometimes we are interested in the auditor's verbal behavior quite apart from any implications that the verbalization may have with respect to the auditor's internal states. Because we tend to confuse verbal behaviors (such as the expression "I hate war") with the internal or subjective states that they are thought to reflect (such as the actual feeling of dislike toward war), we tend to overlook the importance of influence over the auditor's verbal behavior as a desirable outcome of oral communication. We are inclined to say that we are interested in the auditor's verbalizations only as indexes to their internal states, but under some circumstances, it may actually be much more important for listeners to talk about the topic in a certain way than to harbor some particular set of feelings toward it. Very often when speakers say that they want to "inform" their audiences or "convince" them, their actual goal is to influence the auditor's verbal behavior, whether or not they are actually informed or convinced as a matter of subjective fact.

Thus, the object of brain-washing is not necessarily to effect any substantial or immediate change in the victim's way of **thinking,** but to alter his way of **talking.** He then becomes a source of favorable stimulation for others and eventually may even convince himself. If you and I disagree concerning the proper solution to a problem, and I can get you to talk about it in my terms, you will eventually capitulate to my view. If I can keep the entire community **talking** about patriotic themes regardless of how they feel about them, eventually they will whip up a wave of patriotic sentiment.

The interpretation of verbal behavior as an index to subjective states is based upon inference and hence subject to a certain unreliability. But the interpretation of verbal behavior in its own right as a legitimate product response to speaking is a matter of simple observation, and no inference is involved. When Woodrow Wilson coined the expression "Make the world safe for democracy," and when that expression was repeated by others during the succeeding years over and over again in thousands of contexts, the verbalization (quite apart from any sentiment that it might be thought to reveal) could be taken quite legitimately as a product response to Wilson's speaking. A political candidate, advertiser, religious leader, teacher, or revolutionary may well be interested in the frequency with which his verbal formulations are repeated by auditors and auditors-of-auditors when his speech is over. Such influence on their verbalization may be the most powerful and far-reaching effect of his speech.

Sometimes the speaker is interested in the auditor's overt, nonverbal behavior following the speech. The salesman is interested in getting his auditor's signature on a contract. The chemistry laboratory instructor is interested in seeing the student perform a series of manipulations with laboratory materials. The fund-drive speaker is interested in getting the auditor to make a contribution. The politician wants a vote. To be sure, these individuals may sometimes set more limited, "intermediate" goals with certain groups of auditors; the salesman may on a given occasion settle for good will, the laboratory instructor for correct answers to certain questions, the fund-drive speaker for an improved attitude, or the politician for a weakening of opposition. But on some occasions the speaker's real and immediate goal is overt, nonverbal behavior of a particular desired kind.

In this case, too, the speaker is able to observe directly the effects of his speech. No inference is involved in counting votes, sales, contributions, or properly conducted experiments. Of course, this is not to suggest that these behaviors are not accompanied by subjective events, or to imply that the speaker who is looking beyond the immediate speech should fail to note these nonobservables to whatever extent is possible; but to the extent that overt behavior is desired as an outcome of a given speech, no inference is necessary to describe the outcome of the speech; it will be observable, at least in principle.

### Instrumentation

Many of the types of information referred to in the preceding pages can be obtained informally, or through casual observation and inference. For example, the speaker can often obtain enough information about momentary audience interest levels during the speech simply through his unsystematic observation of auditors' overt behavior, and the salesman can keep an informal box-score on proportion of sales as a rough index of the effectiveness of his sales pitch.

However, some kinds of information (such as physiological response data) can be obtained only with the aid of special instruments. Moreover, some situations demand that more formal procedures be used to obtain data that in other situations might be obtained informally. If, for example, a speaker should wish to pretest two alternative forms of a message, and to compare process responses to the two, then it would be wise to have some more reliable basis for comparison of the process effects than his recollection of what happened in the audience during the two speeches. Here, the speaker might want to compare audience analyzer responses, or to analyze pictures of the audience during the speech, or to use some other form of data collection that would produce somewhat more reliable and permanent results. That is, he might prefer to collect his data according to more formal procedures.

We shall refer to any formal procedure for gathering data about auditors as an "instrument," and to the general problem of devising these procedures as the problem of "instrumentation." Although a virtually endless list might be compiled of instruments that are sometimes useful in audience analysis, we shall single out seven types of instruments as being of special significance and collectively representative. These are questionnaires, attitude tests, audience analyzers, information tests, the physiograph, the observation inventory, and content analysis. Some of these apply to the problem of assessing predisposing characteristics, some to process responses, some to product responses, and some to two or more of these. All but three of them are applied exclusively to verbal behavior.

**Questionnaires.** Depending upon how a speaker intends to interpret the results, he may treat a questionnaire as a source of data in its own right or as a means of eliciting verbal behavior that is to be subjected to content analysis.

When used as a means of establishing predisposing characteristics of auditors, it ordinarily is designed to gather demographic information and information relating to the auditor's previous experiences. In preparing a classroom speech on Winston Churchill's eloquence, for example, a student speaker might want to know how many of his auditors were history majors, how many were majoring in English or speech, and so forth. He might also want to know how many of his auditors had even heard a Churchill speech or read one. He might want to collect some supplementary data regarding their knowledge of certain details of World War II, about which some of Churchill's most famous speeches were made. Assuming that he believes that his fellow students will give him truthful replies to his questions, he may obtain the information he requires by asking them to complete a questionnaire.

However, the questionnaire is not limited to a device for gathering demographic and background data on listeners. It may also be used to elicit verbal behavior either before or after the speech in order to estimate predisposing characteristics or product responses. For instance, if a speaker were planning to talk about wiretapping, he might want to know how his audience viewed and evaluated the practice. One approach to getting that information would be to devise a questionnaire consisting of a few leading questions such as, "What do you feel are the strongest arguments against the use of wiretapping by police?" Answers to this question could be analyzed and classified, and the speaker would have a basis for inferring dominant trends of opinion among his auditors.

**Attitude tests.** Popular thinking tends to include along with questionnaires a somewhat more specialized class of instruments called opinion or attitude tests. The purpose of most of these tests is to locate the attitude of the auditor toward a given attitude object at a point on a continuum running from favorable to unfavorable. In its simplest form, the attitude test consists of a single continuous line on which the auditor is asked to place a checkmark corresponding to his feeling about the attitude object. For instance:

What is your attitude toward allowing police to make unlimited use of wiretapping in the investigation of crime?

| Strongly Approve | Approve | Undecided | Disapprove | Strongly Disapprove |
|---|---|---|---|---|
| ——— | ——— | ——— | ——— | ——— |

It is sometimes remarked that single-item tests of this sort are unreliable and subject to momentary fluctuations. As a remedy for this problem, most attitude tests consist of several items clustering around a single topic, and the attitude is taken as the average of the auditor's responses to all of the questions.

A further objection to attitude tests has been raised on the ground that auditors may distort their responses in order to mislead the tester, or to avoid an invasion of their privacy, or for a variety of other reasons. In an effort to overcome these objections, a device called the "semantic differential," which was originally designed for other purposes, has been adapted to audience attitude measurement. Responses to a semantic differential appear to the auditor taking the test to be less revealing of his attitude, and it is presumed that this leads to more candid responses. For instance, the auditor might be asked to check the point on each of the following scales that best represented his evaluation of the attitude object:

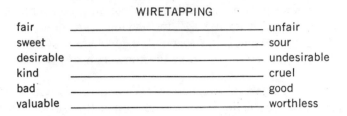

WIRETAPPING

| | | |
|---|---|---|
| fair | _____ | unfair |
| sweet | _____ | sour |
| desirable | _____ | undesirable |
| kind | _____ | cruel |
| bad | _____ | good |
| valuable | _____ | worthless |

Research has shown that an average of the above scales will yield a single score that reflects the auditor's evaluation of wiretapping at least as well as an attitude test of the more conventional type.

It is important to note that the attitude test, though it renders a numerical score, is concerned basically with the auditor's verbal behavior; but, instead of allowing the auditor to formulate his own verbalizations, as in the type of questionnaire that uses leading questions, the verbalizations are formulated by the tester and the auditor is asked merely to indicate his response. If a speaker knows exactly what he is trying to learn about his auditor's attitudes, the attitude test will no doubt render the more precise estimates. However, if he is not quite sure what it is about his auditor's attitudes he needs to know, the speaker should use the less structured approach, for in free verbal response the auditor may tell the speaker something of importance that the speaker would not have thought to ask.

**Audience analyzers.** The audience analyzer has already been discussed in Chapter Three. Its central unit is a device for recording individual responses of auditors as they hear a speech or view a TV program or a play. Each subject has a device for registering his momentary responses. It may be a single button, an array of buttons, a three-way switch, or a dial with several possible settings. He uses the button, switch, or dial to indicate his responses according to some prearranged standard.

For example, the auditor may be asked to use his response recorder to indicate how interesting he finds the speech from moment to moment. If the response recorder is a single button, he may be asked to press the button when he finds the speech interesting, but otherwise leave it alone. Or, if the response recorder is a three-way switch, he may be asked to press the switch to the right when he thinks the speech is interesting, to the left when he thinks it is very dull, and otherwise to leave the switch in the middle. Or, if his response mechanism is a dial with seven possible numbered settings, he may be asked to use "1" to indicate "very dull," "7" to indicate "very interesting," and so on. The number of possible responses he can give is determined by the complexity of the response recorder.

As we have indicated earlier, the audience analyzer is not limited to any particular type of response to the speech (though of course the auditor can record only one type of response at a time). It may be used to measure the auditor's impression of the speech's interestingness, truthfulness, acceptability, or any other quality that the speaker desires.

Again, the audience analyzer uses basically verbal behavior. Although the results appear as tracings or other records that have numerical value, the numbers are based in fact on words, because each of the numbers is defined in terms of the auditor's verbal response to the speech.

**Information tests.** Except for teachers, a speaker seldom has an opportunity to administer information tests to his auditors as a measure of their knowledge before the speech or as a measure of their information gain afterwards. However, speaking to inform has in our technological age become a dominant form of public address, and the documentary has emerged as an important instrument of public service in broadcasting. In planning for and pretesting both informative speeches and documentaries it is helpful to know something about auditor information levels before and after the speech. The best way to get this information is through a test.

Outside of graduate schools of education, the information test is perhaps the most neglected form of instrumentation for audience measurement. It is widely presumed that all such tests measure the same thing but that different forms of tests measure it differently. The fact is that we include a variety of things under the term "knowledge" or "information," although knowledge and information are really quite different from one another.

Different types of tests are required to measure different kinds of knowledge. We may distinguish here among three broad classes of information tests; recognition tests, discrete-item recall tests, and structured recall (or essay) tests.

A recognition test is the familiar "objective," machine-scored examination familiar to undergraduates. The "questions" consist of statements that the auditor is asked to label true or false or of sets of statements from which he is to choose the correct or best one. Ordinarily the proportion of correct answers is used as a single index of the auditor's level of information. There is seldom any effort to specify in which areas of knowledge the auditor is strong and in which he is weak.

The discrete-item recall test is more difficult. Instead of recognizing the correct answer, the auditor must reconstruct it out of his memory. Short-answer and "fill-the-blanks" questions test for this kind of knowledge. Particularly if a person is only casually familiar with a given area of knowledge, he might be able to answer many recognition questions but few recall questions. If, for example, the speaker is interested in teaching his auditors to recognize bogus currency, it will not be sufficient that they can answer "true" to the statement, "On a counterfeit bill, the points on the seal are often broken or bent." On the contrary, the auditor must remember to look for that characteristic on his own initiative. These are clearly two different kinds of knowledge and must be tested for in different ways.

Finally, a speaker may be interested in teaching the auditor to associate various items of information in a particular structure. The items individually may be in fact less important than the structure of ideas within which they are related to one another. Information or knowledge in this sense can be measured only by what we usually call an "essay" test. In the essay test the auditor must pull together various bits of information to construct an extended answer. For example, there is no brief, simple answer to the question, "What were the essential features of Plato's doctrine of ideas?" To answer such a question is complicated because a number of specific elements must be mentioned, and they must be set out in relation to one another. All of the elements could be present, yet the answer still be inadequate if the elements were not properly interrelated.

If a speaker is interested in how well informed his auditors are in the sense of whether they hold certain well-developed concepts, then he will have to test for this information with something like an essay test. To know whether his auditors understand the major causes of juvenile delinquency, or whether they know what makes an internal combustion engine run, or whether they understand the principle of crop rotation, a speaker will have to ask them questions that require them to construct fairly complicated responses.

**Physiographs.** The term "physiograph" is used to refer to any instrument that measures and records one or more physiological responses. As we have seen, these responses are sometimes useful in interpreting process response to communication, and so their instrumentation is important.

The physical responses with which audience analysts are concerned are those that can be measured peripherally—that is, without penetrating into or under the skin. A surprising variety of such processes are available. They include the psychogalvanic skin response (GSR), heart rate, blood pressure, skin temperature, capillary dilation, the palmar sweat response (PSR), gross patterns of activity in the brain, breathing, and covert muscular tensions.

The skin offers some resistance to the passage of a mild electrical current. Under conditions of arousal or stress, this resistance drops markedly. This response of the skin to certain stimuli is what we have called the GSR. By passing a current through the skin and recording its resistance continuously on a strip of graph paper (called a graphic level recorder) we may subsequently correlate the dips in skin resistance with elements of the message being presented at the time.

The heart responds to environmental stimuli by increasing or decreasing its pumping rate and by increasing or decreasing the strength of its contractions. The rate in particular may be measured from an electrocardiogram (EKG), which records the electrical potentials associated with heart action. It may also be recorded by placing a microphone against the chest and recording the amplified sound of the heartbeat. Blood pressure, which results partly from changes in heart action and partly from other factors in the circulatory system, usually is measured in a way that is familiar to most of us from our occasional visits to the doctor. Transduced to an electrical signal and amplified, the measurement can be recorded continuously on a graphic level recorder.

As we know from such experiences as blushing, blanching, hot flashes, and cold sweats, the surface temperature of the skin responds to extreme emotional stimulation. A thermistor, which is a sort of electronic thermometer, may be fixed on the surface of the skin to measure the rather minute temperature differentials that accompany emotional arousal or depression. The resulting skin temperatures may be read from a meter or recorded permanently and continuously on a stripchart recorder.

Probably closely associated with skin temperature, though by no means inflexibly tied to it, is the action of the capillaries. These dilate and contract in response to a great range of stimulation (for example, cigarette smoking usually causes them to contract) including emotionally arousing stimuli. Their dilation may be measured by an electroplethysmograph—a device that uses a photoelectric cell to measure the amount of light passed through the skin from a source of known standard intensity. The amount of light transmitted varies with capillary dilation.

The palms of the hands and soles of the feet perspire in response to emotional stimulation. Through the centuries, sweaty palms have been taken as a sign of anxiety, fear, or great anticipation. In recent times it has become possible to quantify the amount of palmar sweating in several ways and to use the resulting measure as an index of emotional arousal. Perhaps the most satisfactory method of measuring palmar sweating is to seal a small, airtight capsule on the palm and to pass dry air through the capsule and over a sensitive electronic humidity sensor. As the palms sweat, they release moisture into the dry air, and so the humidity of the air reaching the electronic sensor is a direct and continuous measure of palmar sweating.

Patterns of electrochemical activity in the brain may be sensed by electrodes placed on the surface of the scalp. Very useful for diagnosing brain malfunction, these measurements have in recent years been thought to hold possibilities for identifying characteristic patterns attributable to subjective states. The work on "brain waves" as electroencephalograms (or EEG's) are called, is still incomplete. Little is known about the interpretation of EEG patterns produced by auditors while listening to spoken messages.

Breathing, which is deep, slow, and regular during sleep, may become shallow, rapid, or irregular during aroused states. By means of an air-filled tube tied around the chest, it is possible to measure changes in breathing. A device for measuring respiration is called a pneumograph, and its mechanical pressure readings can be transduced into electrical signals and recorded on a stripchart recorder.

Finally, small muscle contractions characterize many states of attention and arousal. These may be measured by recording the electrical potentials that all muscles create when they contract. A small electrode is attached to the surface of the skin, which records the small currents in the muscle immediately below. These tiny potentials can be amplified and recorded in the same manner as other physiological data.

These measurements may be taken separately or several of them may be taken simultaneously and recorded on a single, wide strip of chart paper. An instrument which makes recordings of several physiological responses simultaneously is called a polygraph. The original polygraph was the lie detector, but more sophisticated polygraphs are constantly under development for research into human behavior, including response to communication. Such instruments are useful for measuring process responses, and as we have seen, we still have much to learn about the interpretation of the data they yield.

**Observation inventories.** We have noted that speakers often need to observe overt, nonverbal behavior of auditors either as a means of detecting process responses or as a way of measuring the outcome of the speech. We have noted that most speakers do something of this kind on an informal basis as they talk, but it is also possible to make more systematic observations of auditor behavior by making up in advance lists of behaviors that are to be counted or otherwise observed. Such aids to observation of overt auditor response will be called observation inventories.

The simplest observation inventory is a binary judgment. Did the auditor buy (or vote for me, or contribute money) or not? A box score of such binary judgments over the entire audience is one way to measure the effectiveness of a speech, at least insofar as the speech was designed to produce immediate action.

But more sophisticated inventories are also possible. For instance we might measure attention by the proportion of time that the auditor looks at the speaker. Continuous observation of this single characteristic might be used as a basis for inferring the auditor's overall interest level and the high and low interest points of the speech for him.

Or, a number of more discrete behaviors might be noted. A list of behaviors that are presumed to reflect agreement, for example, might be compiled, and each item noted as it occurred in the auditor's behavioral pattern as he listened to the speech. A similar approach could be taken to the auditor's behavior after the speech to measure some aspects of his response to the whole speech.

**Content analysis.** Content analysis is usually regarded as a means of studying the speaker, not the auditor. By analyzing his messages, we try to make inferences about what the speaker knows and feels, what his attitudes are and how strong they may be, what he is trying to do with his audience, and how he probably will behave in the future. Of course, if we allow auditors to talk or write, then we can apply the same procedures to studying them.

Content analysis may be applied to a variety of verbal materials in order to make estimates about auditors. If we know what newspapers' auditors read, for example, we can analyze the papers. Under some conditions, we may be able to infer that the characteristics of the auditors are similar to the characteristics reflected in the papers. For example, an analysis of the news media of the radical right has been used to interpret the thinking of members of ultraconservative groups that read those newspapers.

We may also apply content analysis to diaries, letters, speeches, or other documents produced by the auditor at an earlier time and to materials elicited for purposes of analysis by the speaker or his aides, such as questionnaire or interview responses.

The essential procedure of content analysis is the establishment of certain categories according to which the contents are analyzed and classified. Depending upon the analyst's purpose, these may be very specific categories, such as, "respondent says private health insurance costs too much" or "respondent says doctor bills are too high." On the other hand, the categories may be very general, such as "respondent expresses negative attitude toward private health plans," or "respondent talks about cost of medical care." Tallies are kept of the frequency of occurrence. From the resulting data it is often possible to construct good estimates of the subject's attention to, knowledge of, and feelings about a particular topic and topics closely related to it.

## Inference from samples

It is rarely, if ever, that the ordinary speaker will be able to apply whatever measuring instruments he chooses to the entire audience. Usually he will have to be satisfied at most with a sample of auditors. Sometimes he will not be able to sample the audience itself but will have to obtain data from other audiences that he presumes to be similar. Sometimes he may have to obtain his information about the audience from even less direct sources. These limitations pose different problems of inference concerning audience response.

If it is possible to apply his measuring instruments to the entire audience, the speaker may have relatively little difficulty generalizing about audience characteristics or response. This will be true particularly if the characteristics or responses of most of the auditors are very similar, but if auditors differ greatly, the speaker may discover that no valid generalizations about them can be made. Under these circumstances, he will either try to find some strategy of communication that will achieve what he desires with diverse auditors, or he will tailor his strategy primarily to some meaningful subgroup of auditors, aiming for maximum effect on them. In short, if auditors are quite diverse, it may not be possible to generalize about them meaningfully even if data concerning all of them are available.

Usually, however, the speaker will not have such a wealth of data available. He will have to work with a sample of auditors, from whose characteristics he will hope to infer certain things about the audience as a whole. In determining audience response to a political speech, for example, party workers sometimes interview samples of auditors after the speech is over. Because of the large crowd and the small number of interviewers, it is generally impossible to interview more than a handful of those present. Under these circumstances, a **random sample** is sometimes possible to obtain.

A random sample is a sample drawn according to principles that guarantee that no single auditor is any more likely to be drawn for the sample than is any other auditor. A random sample gives the most reliable basis for estimating characteristics or responses of the larger audience from which it was drawn.

Sometimes a random sample is not obtainable. Under these circumstances, the speaker or his aides will work with available samples or volunteer samples.

An **available sample** is the group of auditors who happen to be available to the speaker for one reason or another. If, for example, I am to speak at the national convention of a professional society, I may seek to interview local members of the society prior to preparing my speech. The local members are chosen, not because they are a representative sample of the auditors I shall face, but because they are available to me and the others are not. The obvious problem with an available sample is that the very circumstances that make the sample available might contribute to differences in auditor characteristics and response. In the instance cited, the local sample may differ somewhat from the national group as a whole with respect to interests, knowledge, or attitudes.

A **volunteer sample** is a very special kind of available sample. The volunteer sample is composed of people who have come forward to be subjected to whatever measurements the speaker desires. The volunteer often is either a curiosity seeker or someone with his own ax to grind, and as a result his characteristics and his behavior are likely to differ somewhat from those of the ordinary auditor. In interpreting data from volunteer samples, the speaker is well advised to bear in mind the possibility that some of his subjects are perhaps unusually anxious to please, while others are motivated by an abnormally high interest in the topic, perhaps coupled with an extreme positive or negative attitude toward him or his topic.

When no sample of the audience is available, the speaker must collect information from other sources. One possibility is to collect data from an audience that the speaker presumes to be similar in most important respects to the target audience. It is on the basis of this type of reasoning that an instructional film that has worked well with a trial group of students in a particular freshman college course is sold for use in similar courses at other colleges and universities. The presumption is that freshmen are pretty much alike in those respects that govern readiness for and response to the film in question, and therefore that other groups will respond pretty much as the original test group did. Of course, as time passes, freshmen change; so in due course, the film will become obsolete.

Another possibility is to interview somebody who is presumed to be familiar with the audience, perhaps a prominent member of the group that will hear the speech. Reportedly, Eleanor Roosevelt never made a speech to any unfamiliar group without first holding a long discussion with a representative of the group. On the basis of the interview, she was able to infer some of the most prominent characteristics of the group and to anticipate their reactions to alternative ideas and approaches. Producers are interested in what the critics say about their plays—not just because critical attitudes tend to shape public response, but also because the critic's reaction is more likely than the reaction of any other small group of viewers to characterize how the theatre-going public will react. It is obvious that inferences based on opinions and information offered by a single member of the audience are reliable only to the extent that the auditor understands and is typical of the group. Of all members, officers and other prominent group members tend to be most typical of and most knowledgeable about the predisposing characteristics and responses of the group as a whole.

Finally, as we have noted earlier, the speaker can analyze mass media. A newspaper report of his speech may give him some indication of its success; several newspaper reports taken together will give him a good rough picture of what his speech probably meant to the average listener.

Regardless of the source of data, we have seen that inferences about audiences may present difficulties. On the other hand, we have also seen that direct access to the entire audience is not necessary to make some inferences about its predisposing characteristics or its responses to communication.

*Part two*

# SOME GENERAL APPROACHES TO AUDIENCES

# FIVE

# Images in the auditor

For normal human beings the world is neither a gray blur nor a jangling chaos. At the level of conscious experience it consists mostly of an organized set of discriminable objects and a more or less orderly procession of discrete events. The individual locates himself in space with reference to the objects and in time with reference to the events, and thus develops a representation of what the world is like and how he fits into it. This representation of the world is composed of what he knows and believes, and it forms the basis of his intellectual style. Because that style controls in large measure how he responds to incoming messages, it is essential to describe certain features of it if we are to understand the effects of communication.

## The organization of experience

The origin of one's representation of the world around him is found in sense impressions. As I sit at my typewriter, I am bombarded by innumerable stimuli in many forms. I hear a faint clicking sound repeated at regular intervals. A pungent fragrance fills the air. A very complex pattern of colored light lies just before my eyes, and it is altered as I shift my gaze. When I turn one way the pattern changes and the light gets brighter; if I turn the other, the pattern changes in another way and the light dims. There is an irregular, rasping sound at intervals. One at a time, in no particular order, my fingertips feel a firm pressure.

But this way of speaking of my experience of the world around me is, to say the least, unusual; and, except for a certain school of modern writers, it would be regarded as utterly bizarre. With the possible exception of early infancy, experience does not come to us as a jumble of disconnected stimuli; on the contrary, ordinarily we organize our experience in a meaningful way. I hear my clock ticking on the wall. I smell the familiar fragrance of my brand of pipe tobacco. On the table before me I see my typewriter, a stack of paper on which I am going to write, and some books. I turn toward the window and see the spice tree in my back yard bathed in the morning sun. When I turn away from the window, I see the shaded interior of the room with its chairs, lamps, tables, and bookshelves. A Florida Jay is in the tree outside, chattering furiously. As I type this page, I feel my fingertips striking the surface of the keys. I know where I am, what I am doing, and what is going on around me. My experience is organized.

When we say that experience is organized, we mean that separate stimuli are linked to other stimuli, past and present, in such a fashion that the occurrence of one leads us to infer or predict the occurrence of others. Just how we learn to make such connections is an interesting question that is beyond the scope of our present purpose, but it is important to notice that for each of us experiences become organized around certain foci. That is, the innumerable stimuli to which we are subjected are not randomly connected with one another but are clustered around a much smaller number of central nodes.

For example, a good deal of the experience of most contemporary Americans is organized around a node that carries the label "The Automobile." They can identify one when they see it and differentiate several species (station wagon, limousine, sport racer, and so forth) and several more varieties (Chevrolet, Porsche, Cadillac, Lotus, and so forth). Many Americans have fairly good understandings of such related terms as "carburetor," "distributor," "differential," and "torsion-bar." They know the difference between a heap and a creampuff. They know about such mishaps as blowouts, vapor locks, sideswipes, and fender benders. They know that many people die each year as a result of riding in automobiles and that each time they get in one they are taking a small risk of injury and a smaller risk of death. They also know that a group calling itself the National Safety Council worries a lot about bad driving habits and that traffic officers spend their working days apprehending drivers who violate certain specified standards of driving practice caller "traffic laws." Americans know that a large part of their prosperity rests upon the manufacture and sale of cars. They associate the use of a car with the expenditure of large sums of money; yet they also associate its use with profit, convenience, pleasure, and a sense of liberation. They know that it is sometimes hard to find a place to put one when you are not riding in it; they call this "the parking problem." Now, these experiences and ideas are varied, but they are not miscellaneous, for in one way or another they all are related to each other through a single, organizing concept, "the automobile."

We have spoken of "the automobile" as a concept. As a matter of fact, the term "concept" frequently is used to refer to rather specific and fairly well-defined ideas. In this sense, the **concept** of "the automobile" includes only those aspects of automobiles that are directly related to the object itself; such associated ideas as "traffic officer," "car pool," and "death on the highways" would be regarded as related concepts, but not as part of the concept itself.

However, in our discussions here we will want to talk about any complex of associations surrounding a common focus or node, including all of the associations that would ordinarily be encompassed within a concept, but also including any other related associations whatsoever. For this purpose we shall use the term "image." The **image** of a thing is the complex of associations that it arouses within an individual. An image exists within the mind of a given individual, and it is subject to change; therefore, what is or is not a part of the image is always dependent on a given auditor at a given time. Thus, "beautiful," "V-8," "expensive," "piston," "turnpike," and "car pool" are all elements of a single image, a single cluster of associations, for many Americans. "The automobile" is the label given to the point of focus or node around which these associations are clustered. For others, or for the same individuals at another time, some of these elements may be missing from the image.

## Functional aspects of images

Not only do images differ from one another with respect to their contents, but they differ also with respect to the way in which they operate within the auditor's conceptual system. Of these functional differences four are especially important: clarity, salience, coherence, and integration.

**Clarity.** Images differ from one another along a dimension running from clear to vague. For example, my image of the English language is very clear. Not only can I use it as a speaker and listener, but I have considerable other information about it. I know that, according to one popular analysis of the language, its words are classed as parts of speech such as verb, noun, and preposition. I know that the verbs have tenses and moods, that the nouns have cases, and the like. I also know that this analysis of the language has been challenged by structural linguists, and I know on what grounds it has been challenged. I know the sounds of the language, its rhythm and melody, and something of its history. I know many more things about the English language, including the fact that it belongs to a family of languages called Indo-European, and that one of these languages is Sanskrit.

But my image of Sanskrit is quite vague. I do not know a single word of Sanskrit. I do know that it is very old, much older than English, but how much older I am not sure. I think, but I am not sure, that it is involved in the Hindu religion in a way that is somewhat similar to the way Latin is involved with the Catholic church. I do not know how it sounds; in fact, I am not certain that anybody still speaks it. I have the impression that only very scholarly people read it, and I think it might be rather hard to learn. When I hear of it, I think of minarets and turbaned gentlemen in long robes, but I realize this association is romantic. I once saw a sample of written Sanskrit, and I recall that its alphabet is much different from ours, but I don't actually remember what any of the symbols looked like. And that just about covers what I know about Sanskrit: I can say very few things about it, and to most of those things I have to add "maybe," or "I think," or "but I could be wrong." By contrast, I can say a great many things about English, most of which I am quite sure about. My image of English is quite clear; my image of Sanskrit is extremely vague.

We need to bear in mind that the clarity of an image has nothing to do with its accuracy. For example, there are no doubt some errors in my image of English, points on which I am utterly confident of my knowledge but on which I am completely in error. When we speak of the clarity of an image, we are talking about how it appears to the individual who holds it, not how accurate it is when judged by an external criterion. An individual may correct an error in his image, but until he corrects it, he will behave as if it were true.

**Salience.** For a given individual at a particular time, some images come to mind more readily than others. For each of us there are some images that leap to mind at the slightest provocation or the remotest association, and others that are dragged into awareness only by repeated stimulation. Those images that are, so to speak, in the forefront of a person's mind are for him said to be salient, while those that are evoked with difficulty are said to be latent.

Astronomy, bureaucracy, the civil rights movement, theory, and parochialism are images that are for me very salient. I think of each of these topics quite often, sometimes in what would to anybody else appear to be completely unrelated contexts, and I invariably think of them when a closely associated topic is under discussion. In a group, I am frequently the first person to mention one of these topics and to relate it to the topic of conversation. When a speaker is leading up to one of these topics, I am among the first of his auditors to sense that he is doing so.

On the other hand, Monaco, extrasensory perception, Zen Bhuddism, the Civil War, and modern jazz are images that are for me pretty latent. I do not think of these things very often, and in a speech or discussion these or similar topics might be under discussion for some time before I would realize it. If a speaker referred indirectly to one of these topics, I might very well fail to notice that he had done so.

Although there might be some tendency for clear concepts to be salient also, this is not generally so. For example, I know roughly as much about extrasensory perception as I do about astronomy, and I have read several books and many articles on the topic; yet astronomy is salient and extrasensory perception is latent for me.

Moreover, salience should not be confused with valuation. The fact that an image is salient does not mean that it is favorable. For example, I regard bureaucracy in a very poor light; yet it is an image that is easily evoked in me, hence salient. Santa Claus, on the other. hand, has a very favorable image for me; yet it is an exceedingly latent one.

**Coherence.** We have defined an image as a cluster of associations around a common node, but images differ with respect to the internal harmony that this cluster displays. In some images, all of the elements and associations add up to a unified and harmonious impression in which there are no loose ends or dissident elements. An image that displays such internal harmony is said to be **coherent.** But in other images there are ambiguities and conflicting implications. An image that displays internal conflict is said to be **dissonant.**

For example, my image of Napoleon is quite coherent. He was brilliant, vain, powerful, idolized by his followers, and a warmonger. Nothing I know about him contravenes any of these elements, nor do they conflict with one another. Indeed, such a combination of characteristics is not at all unlikely. On the other hand, my image of George Washington has recently become quite dissonant. I have always regarded Washington as a wise, modest, careful, self-sacrificing statesman, something of a father figure. However, I have recently read in a reliable source that Washington consorted with barmaids. This does not fit well with the rest of my knowledge about Washington. Until I can obtain additional information that will explain the discrepancy, or find some basis for discrediting the information I have recently received, or locate a rationalization that will allow these impressions to co-exist, my image of Washington will be a dissonant one.

Dissonance arises from the presence in the image of elements having conflicting implications or from recognized and unresolved ambiguities. Again it is important to realize that the conflict and the ambiguity that produce dissonance in an individual's image are those that he himself recognizes, not those that would be obvious to an outsider.

**Integration.** Images are connected with other images. For most of us, "university" is connected with student, with education, with faculty, and with many other images. Some images are connected with a very large number of other images within the individual's conceptual system, and these are called **integrated.** Other images are connected to very few other images within the individual's conceptual system, and these are called **isolated.**

For most adults in Europe and America, Hitler is associated with World War II, genocide, Herman Goering, fascism, Krupp, V-2 rocket, the battle of Stalingrad, and numerous other concepts. Within their conceptual systems, the image of Hitler is integrated because it is connected with a sizable number of other images. Mention Hitler, and many of these things come to mind. Bring any of these images to mind, and Hitler is likely to come along. On the other hand, Syngman Rhee is for most of them a rather isolated image. They know he was for many years the Korean head of state, but they do not connect him with many other things.

For me, "philosophy" is a concept that is well integrated in my conceptual system; I connect it with many other things in a very definite way. But I recognize that for most people, philosophy is a fairly isolated concept; they tend to think of it as a separate thing, apart from most other considerations. The mention of philosophy does not bring a crowd of other images to mind, and there are few other images the mention of which will bring philosophy to mind.

## Images and messages

An auditor carries his images with him into the listening situation. Whatever effect the message has upon him will occur through stimulation of that set of images, and some of the most profound effects of communication may take place in the image system itself. It is, therefore, important to note some characteristics of the way in which images interact with incoming messages.

To begin with, it is important to bear in mind that, although the speaker has control of stimuli that he intends to present to the auditor, he does not have control over what images will be aroused by those stimuli. Words and tones that produce one image in the speaker may produce a totally different image in the auditor.

For example, the word "bullfight" arouses in most Spaniards images widely differing from those it arouses in most Americans. For one thing, the contents of images will differ to a very great extent. When he thinks of the bull, the typical American will see in his mind's eye a fat, domesticated, stupid, phlegmatic, but ill-tempered beast—a Hereford or an Angus. When the Spaniard thinks of the bull, he sees a Miura, a lean, wild, powerful, sure-footed, and courageous animal. In his thinking the American links the idea of bullfighting with bearbaiting or cockfights, a cheap and cruel thrill. The typical Spaniard links the idea of bullfighting to tragedy and high drama, a pageant of the human spirit dating to ancient times. The Spaniard, of course, has a much clearer and more integrated image; for him the spectacle is divided into discrete acts, each with its own proprieties and meaning. He recalls great matadors of the past like Manolete and Dominguin, and he looks for reflections of their styles in the performances of younger men.

Even where the elements of the image are the same, their organization is quite different in different people, especially with respect to which elements are salient and which latent, so that the resulting images are different even where we might expect them to be the same. The American might say that in a bullfight a man in a shiny costume uses a cape to lure a bull into a position where he can stab it to death with a sword. Although all of the elements necessary to form this impression are present for the Spaniard, he would have difficulty recognizing this as a description of the **corrida;** he would say that if nothing more than this were to happen it would be a waste of a Sunday afternoon and a good bull. He would say that in a bullfight a man brings himself as close as possible to death on the horns of an angry bull, pitting skill and nerve against brute strength and courage. To the American, the salient features of the image are blood and death. In the face of what he regards as senseless slaughter, he has trouble appreciating the matador's skill or the courage of the bull; to the Spaniard, these are the salient features of the contest, and the death of the bull is a sad but necessary by-product.

Any stimulus, then, that invokes the image of bullfighting will arouse substantially different impressions in the minds of the American and the Spaniard. It is not just a question of their evaluating the spectacle differently. They actually see in it different objects, events, and abstract properties, and even when some of the elements are shared, they are so organized as to produce quite different images for the two. Only if they recognized these differences in their images could a typical American and a typical Spaniard talk to one another meaningfully about bullfighting.

It would be possible to regard this case as an example of the difficulty of communicating across cultural barriers. We all know that it is difficult for a German to talk to an Italian and more difficult for him to talk to a Chinese; and we are able to recognize the source of much of this communication difficulty in discrepancies between the image systems from one culture to another. But it is only through a conscious effort that we realize that similar differences are to be found much closer to home.

Consider the PTA. Each of us has some image of it, but the features that it contains and their relative degrees of importance in the image differ greatly from one person to another. For example, many PTA leaders have an image of the organization as the main bulwark of the schools and the leading protector of American youth, a supporter of the teacher and a friend of the child. They see it as large and powerful but impartial and thoroughly informed. From this position of benevolent wisdom and strength, they see the organization as a provider of basic information to parents, teachers, legislators, and the public at large, and as an agitator for worthwhile and necessary programs of child welfare and educational growth.

This, however, is only one of many common images of the PTA. For example, many school administrators regard the PTA as an instrument of parental intervention in the affairs of the school. They, too, regard it as large and powerful, but as relatively uninformed and subject to extreme bias. Its value is limited largely to rare intervals of support for public proposals regarding education, such as increasing teacher salaries. To many a school administrator the salient feature of his image of the PTA is the picture of an aroused parent committee seeking changes of school policy which, if granted, would wreck an expertly contrived scheme for matching overpowering needs with scarce resources.

Other prevalent images of the PTA might be cited: the political conservative's view, the anxious parent's view, and so on. But perhaps enough has been said to underscore the point that even within the same community different people hold much different images of such a widely-known and relatively noncontroversial thing as the PTA. They differ with respect to image content and also with respect to image organization. It follows that, when talking about the PTA or when using it as an example or illustration or for purposes of comparison or contrast, the speaker must know something of his audience's image of the organization in order to predict the effects of alternative strategies of communication.

**Effects of images on messages.** Images affect response to incoming messages in three ways: They influence attention, interpretation, and acceptance.

In general, messages dealing with salient images receive a higher degree of attention and receive it more readily than messages dealing with relatively latent images. This applies not only with respect to the major topic under discussion, but also with respect to the images that are brought to bear in dealing with that topic. In other words, we might expect a speech on coeducational dormitories to receive greater initial attention from a randomly assorted group of college students than a speech on hairstyles in the 1920's.

We would also suspect that for these students the former would provide more interesting supporting materials than the latter for a speech on some other topic. A message dealing with any topic, even a dull one, may be received with considerable attention if its content is supported by salient images. The auditor will respond with heightened attention to the salient images when they are presented; and if they are associated with the topic, the topic itself will acquire some of the features and some of the attention value of the supporting images. Usually a speaker does not speak on a topic that is of very low interest to his audience; but on those occasions when he does, it is especially important for him to use whatever knowledge he can get concerning the relative saliency of images that might be connected in some way with his topic.

Images affect attention to incoming messages in another way: They serve to direct the attention of the auditor to certain features of the message as opposed to others. The salient features of an image are those to which the auditor's attention goes first, and they tend to characterize the image for him. One wonders what features must dominate a Frenchman's image of cabbage that permit him to speak of a woman he loves as "my little cabbage." Frankly, a woman who is like a cabbage would not be very appealing to me, but there can be no doubting the Frenchman's intent to flatter his sweetheart by such an expression. His first impressions when he thinks of cabbage are no doubt different from mine.

Because salient features of an image tend to dominate an auditor's response to the image, it is important for the speaker to know what features are salient in order to predict where the auditor's attention will go. Suppose, for example, that a speaker were trying to argue that union leadership should not be hedged about with undue restrictions and that a relatively free hand is necessary if the greatest benefit to the workers is to be attained. He might cite the growth and power of the Teamster's Union and the increase of teamster income during the free-wheeling administration of James Hoffa as an example of what can be done under the right circumstances. For some audiences, this illustration might be appropriate because the very features the speaker wanted to emphasize would be the dominant aspects of the Hoffa image for them. But for most American audiences in the 1960's, this illustration would be extremely unfortunate. It is not just a case of giving tacit approval to a public figure who is generally regarded with great disfavor; the example of Hoffa would call to mind the possibility of misusing the very broad powers that it was the speaker's intent to make appear desirable to the auditors. Flagrant misuse of power in the absence of restraints is, whether justifiably or not, a salient feature of the Hoffa image and therefore almost certain to accompany the arousal of the Hoffa image in most auditors. Although the speaker would hope to discount the likelihood of such misuse of power, the example would direct auditor attention to an aspect of the proposal that the speaker might hope would remain unemphasized.

Earlier in this chapter we have had occasion to notice that images also affect the auditor's interpretation of incoming messages. What he thinks the speaker has said about Hemingway, for example, when the speaker says that Hemingway enjoyed bullfights, depends very much on his image of bullfighting. What he thinks the speaker is saying about a proposal when the speaker says that that proposal was sponsored by the PTA depends very much on the auditor's image of the PTA.

The significance of this point about images is not generally understood. Generally it is thought to mean that, if the speaker is to achieve his desired effect upon an auditor, he must understand certain features of his auditor's image system. This is, of course, true; but even more important, it means that, if the speaker does not understand the auditor's image system, he cannot understand fully what he is saying to the auditor when he makes any statement, whether calculated to produce some particular effect or not.

It is not just a question of whether the auditor develops some particular attitude toward the topic of the speech. It is a question of what "information" he will carry away from his encounter with the speaker. For if my image of sports cars includes high speed as a necessary component, then when you tell me that the British love sports cars I am likely to hear you say that the British love fast cars. If your image of burlesque is roughly equivalent to your image of strip tease, then when I tell you that a certain movie is a burlesque you are likely to believe that I have told you that some things happen in it that, in fact, do not.

Moreover, if the auditor's image is vague and the speaker's image is clear, the speaker is likely to believe that he has given the auditor some information that the auditor has not received. If I tell you that a whippet is like a small greyhound, I may have given you much or little information depending upon how clear is your image of greyhounds. If my own image of them is quite clear, then I may feel that I have given you a great deal of information about the whippet, when I might have given you none at all. What I said was rich in information; what you heard was devoid of it. Examples such as this are usually given as proof of the importance of spelling out your meanings in detail. As a matter of fact, they merely prove the importance of knowing your auditor's images. If the auditor shares your image of the greyhound, you achieve great economy and perhaps a gain in accuracy by using the analogy rather than spelling out the whippet's features in specific detail.

Images also affect what we might call the auditor's acceptance of the message. If you tell most people that you put your hand into a flame and pulled it out unburned, they would reject your statement as false, for it is too greatly at variance with their images of fire and of the human body. Moreover, their images of both of these things are clear and coherent, so that they would have no hesitation about rejecting the claim, even though their image of fire is inaccurate and your statement might very well be true. Before you could make them believe that you had done this, you would have to change their image of fire. Among educated people this would be very easy to do, for you could rely upon their knowledge that various combustible substances burn at different temperatures, and then point out that the flame into which you thrust your hand was produced by burning a substance with an extremely low combustion point.

Among primitive people you would have serious difficulty explaining what you had done, and if they saw you do it, they would prefer an explanation based on a supernatural explanation growing out of images they already have.

This example illustrates two points of importance. First, a message that is incompatible with a clear and coherent image is very likely to be rejected as false, even if it is true. Second, a message that is compatible with a clear and coherent image is likely to be accepted uncritically, even if it is false.

It is important to note that the working of this principle depends upon the clarity and coherence of the image in the mind of the auditor. Thus, when Senator Joseph McCarthy in the 1950's accused minor public officials of Communist sympathies, the accusations were believed by many people, because the image of the Senator as a hard-hitting anti-Communist was clear, and the images of the minor figures he attacked were vague. It was easier to believe that they were indeed Communists than to believe that a United States senator was lying. But when he accused top government officials of the same thing, his claims were rejected by most of those who had supported him before. The images of some of the people attacked were even better established than the Senator's; it was easier to believe that the charges were false. The image of President Eisenhower, for example, was completely incompatible with the charge that he was a "willing tool of the Communist conspiracy."

**Effect of messages on images.** The relationship between messages and images is not unilateral. We have seen that images affect the reception of messages, but it is also true that messages affect the content of images. In fact, some of the most significant effects of communication are those that occur in the auditor's image system. Some of the prominent goals of public speaking are best expressed in terms of the intended effect of the speech on the listener's images and whether the speaker intends it or not, some such effects are likely to occur as a result of any public speech. Messages can create new images, alter old ones, and form new connections among them.

The exact mechanisms by which images become linked to other images are not fully known, but at least two types of connection are very common: contiguity and communality.

Two images may be presented simultaneously or in immediate

succession on a number of occasions. This repeated **contiguity of occurrence** often is sufficient to establish an association between the two. Thus, if a person sees a number of television commercials in which the image of cigarette smoking is repeatedly presented in a context that also includes the image of personal attractiveness, eventually he will tend to develop a positive connection between the two. Negative connections are also possible.

At the time of this writing, an advertising campaign is underway that seems to have as its ultimate goal the elimination of a negative connection that prevents the sale of cigars to women. The advertising series began with a very attractive and unquestionably feminine actress singing a song about a particular brand of cigars and making a short sales pitch apparently directed to male viewers. This was an unusual bit of advertising, for cigar commercials had almost always been done by male announcers and actors before.

Several months later, the actress began to show signs of enjoying the smell of the smoke as a male actor lit up a cigar. Still later, she appeared in commercials in which, in place of the wrapped box of cigars that she had displayed previously, she displayed a single, unwrapped but still unlighted cigar that she passed beneath her nose with manifestations of great pleasure. If this trend should run its full course, the next step should be her holding a lighted cigar, then later on her taking a puff from a male companion's cigar, and finally having her light and smoke a small cigar of her own.

At the time of this writing, such a prospect would seem quite unacceptable to men and women alike, for the image of the cigar is distinctively masculine in our culture (though not in Cuba or Scandinavia). Even in our society of relatively unspecialized sex roles, a woman smoking a cigar would be greeted by shock or laughter, for broad as it is the feminine image leaves no leeway for what is to us now so traditionally masculine an act. The cigar and the adult male have been linked by repeated co-occurrence of the two images in the same context; contiguity of occurrence has developed an association. The purpose of this series of commercials seems to be to weaken that association by gradually insinuating the feminine image into the picture; first as window-dressing for the commercial, then by successive degrees closer and closer to the image of the cigar itself. It is possible that by the time this book appears in print, occasional cigar smoking by women will be regarded by many television viewers as a daring, but not an impossible or socially devastating thing to do. An old connection between images will have been weakened, and a new connection established, entirely by messages.

Incidentally, in the process, a temporary connection between cigar smoking by women and avant-garde thinking will also have been established, for the notion of breaking outworn taboos is itself a powerfully attractive image for many people in our time. Women and girls in this group will try to cultivate an interest in cigar smoking, and young men in this group will look for cigar-smoking girls to date. It is even possible that among this group cigar-smoking will become a symbol of identification with the group, an indispensable element of the image.

Should these events transpire, the participants in it will of course offer rational explanations for their behavior; but insofar as their images are concerned, the relevant connections will have been altered as a result of contiguity. However, connections may also rest upon **communality of elements.** If some of the elements of one image are understood to be also salient elements of another image, then the two will tend to be associated. Thus, for many people, the image of Botticelli and that of Leonardo da Vinci are associated, not because they had any close contact with one another, or because of repeated contiguity, but because the images of the two men contain very many identical elements. If the speaker should mention one of them, auditors who know about both are easily led to think about the other.

Whereas it is a long-term proposition to establish a connection between images through contiguity, it is possible to establish or strengthen with relative ease a connection based on communality. The speaker has merely to know what elements of the two images his auditor holds in common and to focus on those common elements. Indeed, focusing on their common elements will strengthen the association between two images whether it is the speaker's intent to do so or not. Thus many recent messages in the mass media have linked the use of migrant labor to the idea of slavery by focusing on those elements of the two images that are common: poor living and working conditions for the workers, lack of voice in decisions affecting the worker himself, occasional cruelty, and the like. The fact that the migrant worker system is not slavery, and that any employer who tried to behave as if it were would very soon be in serious difficulty, is quite beside the point; by dwelling upon their common aspects, the image of the one can be linked with the image of the other. Moreover, this can be accomplished in a single speech or television documentary and does not require repeated stimulation either for its establishment or for its retention by the auditor.

One way of describing what has happened in the cigar and the migrant worker examples is to say that connections among images have been changed. Another way is to say that the images of "The Cigar" and "The Migrant Worker System" have themselves been changed by messages that have altered the way in which these images are integrated into the auditor's conceptual system. Both statements are true, for anything that changes the integration of an image represents at least some change in the image itself. In the two examples that we have cited, the change was substantial.

Messages also may change images by increasing their salience or clarity or by increasing or decreasing their coherence. Probably any message that arouses an image will increase its salience. Indeed, a message that evokes an image might be said in psychological terms to represent a reinforcement of that image—we retain images that we use and forget images that our environments give us no occasion to employ.

In all probability any message that treats of a particular image serves to improve its clarity; certainly it is difficult to imagine a message that would increase the vagueness of an image. What we usually call "the informative speech" is designed largely to clarify some particular image of the auditor's. A speech on "The Mitochondrion," for example, would probably be designed to change the auditor's image of that organ of the living cell by adding detail to his image of it; that is, by clarifying his image of the mitochondrion. If the speaker knew what details were already part of the auditor's image, he could design a speech that would achieve maximum addition of clarity to the image within the limits of the available time, energy, and resources.

Messages also change images by making them more or less coherent. Any message that resolves a conflict or reinforces a congruity in the auditor's image will enhance its coherence; any message that introduces a conflict will tend to make the image more dissonant. When many people are told that the North Vietnamese

Communist leader, Ho Chi Minh, is very fond of little children and loves to prattle with them and feed them sweets, they find the information difficult to believe because it is so greatly at variance with their image of Ho as a bloodthirsty and doctrinaire revolutionary. If they receive this information on unimpeachable authority, they will accept it grudgingly, but it does not rest comfortably in their image of the man. In this instance, the message has introduced dissonance into what was before a rather coherent image. Sometimes this is precisely what a speaker wishes to do; recognizing that the image is too clear and congruent to allow for a complete reversal as a result of one message, the speaker may elect to introduce one or two dissonant elements. If he does not try to do too much at once, his credibility may remain high enough to permit him to plant the seeds of a fundamental image change, to be nurtured and cultivated at a later time.

Suppose that a speaker has done just this with respect to Ho's image for a particular group of auditors. Their image, which before was coherent and quite unfavorable, is now dissonant and mixed. The man who has planned terrorist raids and guerilla attacks is also perceived to be gentle and kind to children. The groundwork has now been laid for a dramatic reversal of the image. A number of possible factors might account for coexistence of these apparently contradictory facts, one of which is that both of these elements in Ho's nature stem from the same basic cause. The speaker might try to show that Ho's hatred of European powers stems directly from his love of the children of his homeland, for whom he was determined to secure a free and promising future. He might argue that the guerilla's hatred of all factors standing in the way of this dream was so great that he was determined to use any means, however distasteful, to rid his country of these exploiters of the children of North Vietnam. If accepted, this explanation would make the image of Ho Chi Minh clearer by adding detail and would restore coherence to what had become a very dissonant image, but the new image would also be more favorable to the man than the old one.

Perhaps the most important question a speaker can ask himself about his audience's image of his topic is whether their image is already formed, or whether he will be building it from the beginning. If the auditors already have an image, then it is important to know its contents and organization; but if they do not, then it is possible for the speaker to decide what contents he wants the image to have, which elements of the image he wants to make salient, how he will achieve coherence and avoid dissonance, and how he will integrate it into the auditor's cognitive system. With respect to the last point particularly, he will need to know whether images with which he wants to link his topic are held by the auditor, and whether the elements of those images are present that would make it possible to form the sort of connections he desires. The auditor must know something before he can be taught anything.

**Image systems of auditor groups.** Up to this point we have spoken exclusively of "the auditor," but the speaker ordinarily is confronted not by a single auditor but by a group of them. The key question about an auditor group is to what extent its members share their images in common. Probably no two people share all of their images in common, and probably no two people are without any images in common. But between these impossible extremes, what sort of situation is a speaker likely to encounter?

To begin with, the fact that people are together in a group suggests that they have some images in common. Particularly if they are members of an organized group with regular meetings, they are likely to have come to see some aspects of the world in a similar way; also, their presence at the group meeting will make the images they share with that group salient for the time being, hence fairly reliable grounds from which to understand their image systems. In other words, the common image system of the group may be used with some reliability to estimate probable reactions of its individual members on any occasion in which their membership in the group is emphasized. There are certain images that are very salient for members of a particular religious organization, social group, civic club, professional society, or other association. If the speaker can understand those images, he will understand much about his individual auditors, however much they may differ in other respects, because of the salience of their group images when in the group.

For example, unions promulgate a salient, clear, coherent and integrated image that might be labeled "The Brotherhood of Labor." Though on other occasions a union member might backslide and fail to maintain that image clearly before him, at the union meeting that image is very easily aroused in the ordinary member. The speaker who does not understand that image will have considerable trouble communicating with union groups about any matter that is remotely associated with it. There are certain images that are salient at meetings of the PTA, Rotary, the American Association of University Professors, and the Society for the Prevention of Cruelty to Animals. The speaker is well advised to learn as much as possible about the dominant images of the group he is addressing.

It is probably also true that certain dominant images are associated with demographic characteristics, which is perhaps the principal factor making demographic audience analysis useful at all. Age, sex, social class, occupation, religious, and political groups all seem to carry certain images in common. A speaker can depend upon a computerman for certain images that are not widespread among the population at large; the same is true of a suburban teenager, a Cuban refugee, a member of the Pentecostal Church, a college student, a single girl, or a member of the American Nazi Party.

Exclusive groups make some effort to protect their image systems from becoming part of the public domain, with the result that full and free communication with members of such groups is possible only if the speaker should happen to be a member of the group himself. However, in this day of rapid mass communication and public curiosity about any group that is at all remarkable, this battle to prevent the vulgarization of the image system is growing harder to fight. Consequently, information is becoming easier to obtain concerning the images of all groups.

# SIX

# The auditor as reflective thinker

Earlier we noted that our daily lives are governed to a large extent by habit. By the same token, our collective activities in government and organizations are determined largely by routine. Individual habit and organization routine are similar in that they imply fairly standard responses to anticipated stimuli. But occasionally we are confronted with a situation where the habitual responses do not work or else with an entirely new stimulus configuration for which we have no conditioned responses or established routines. In lower forms of life, such as the flatworm, the beetle, or even the rat, response under such novel conditions appears to be mostly random; in man, however, individually and collectively, novel conditions are thought to call forth intelligent decision-making.

Some of the world's leading philosophers and scientists have devoted much effort to the question, "What do men do when they make rational decisions?" None of the answers have proven entirely satisfactory, but particularly useful to the audience analyst is the answer given by John Dewey, who described intelligent human problem-solving as "the reflective thinking process." According to Dewey, when a rational being is confronted with a perplexing situation, he tends to go through certain characteristic stages in reaching a solution. Although Dewey described an elaborate thirteen-step process, we may for our purposes abbreviate it to six main operations, which may be illustrated by the following improbable example:

1. **Felt need or difficulty.** Imagine a man walking down a forest path. He is executing a routine pattern of behavior, putting one foot in front of the other and following the track. Now suppose he rounds a corner and sees that a tree has fallen across the path. It now seems impossible to follow the old routine; he has become aware of a difficulty.

2. **Definition of problem.** At this point the traveler may say to himself, "A tree has been felled across my path and I can no longer continue the way I've been going. I will have to find some way to get by this tree." In so saying, he has formulated his problem in verbal terms. As we shall see presently, this stage of reflective thinking is by no means as trivial as it may seem.

3. **Data collection and analysis.** Now he may begin to look about and to notice some features of the situation. He may note that the tree extends twenty feet to the left and forty feet to the right, that it is eight feet in girth and comes clear to the ground. He may note that to the left, where the roots are, there's swampy ground and to the right it is dry but the branches are spread over a wide area. In short, he tries to collect some information about the situation that might be relevant to deciding what he should do.

4. **Listing alternate solutions.** What courses of action are open to him? He could go back to camp, get a shovel, and dig a tunnel under the tree. He could cut a sapling, strip off the branches, and pole vault over. He could build a fire against the trunk and wait for it to burn through. He could walk around to the left or walk around to the right. Ridiculous as some of them seem, any of these actions would solve the problem as stated.

5. **Identifying criteria for a solution.** Some of the proposed solutions are unacceptable, not because they will not solve the problem, but because they are inefficient or create more problems than they solve; that is, they do not live up to acceptable criteria for a solution to this problem. They are too bothersome, too time-consuming, too dangerous, or they require too much effort. The traveler may say to himself, "I want to adopt the quickest, easiest, safest solution that will permit me to keep my feet dry." In so doing, he has listed his criteria for a solution.

6. **Adopting a solution.** Using the data accumulated in Step 3,

along with the criteria listed in Step 5, he now selects from the list drawn up in Step 4 the best solution. Because he wants to avoid work, he probably will decide not to go back to camp for a shovel or to strip a sapling; because he is in a hurry, he probably will not build a fire; because he wants dry feet, he probably will not go the shorter route to the left; because it is relatively quick, easy, and dry, he probably will circle to the right.

In all likelihood individuals and groups rarely follow exactly this sequence of events in solving problems; that is why we have called them "operations" rather than "steps" in the process. But the more complicated the problem, the more likely it is that all of the operations will have to be performed in order to find the most acceptable solution. By "acceptable" we do not mean "correct" in some moral or logical sense, but simply the solution that the individual or group in question is likely to regard as best in light of their experience and desires.

Because it relates decisions to knowledge and desires, the reflective thinking process can be a valuable tool of audience analysis. By considering which of the operations in this process a group of auditors is likely to have gone through, and how they have managed each of them, a speaker should be able to gain considerable insight into how the group of listeners have thought about the problem. This in turn leads to useful estimates of the likely effects upon them of various kinds of speech content.

Although it is useful for other types of speaking as well, audience analysis based on the reflective thinking process is particularly valuable for understanding how audiences respond to communication that analyzes a problem or recommends a course of action. In predicting response to such communication it is important to know whether the auditors are aware that a problem exists, whether they see it clearly (i.e., as the speaker does), how much information they have about it, whether they are aware of all the possible solutions, what criteria they are using for evaluating solutions to the problem, and whether they have committed themselves to the support of a particular course of action.

**Does the audience know a problem exists?** Sometimes a speaker must communicate to an audience that simply is unacquainted with the topic and is not aware that a problem exists at all. On such occasions, the speaker must decide how far through the process it is possible and desirable to carry the audience in a single speech. Will he try to carry them all the way through the process to a solution, thus accomplishing the entire process of persuasion in a single step? Should he be satisfied to do the best possible job of showing them the existence of a problem? Or should he try for something between these two goals?

Perhaps the commonest, though not necessarily the most effective, approach to such an audience is the "problem—solution" speech. Usually it is so designed that the first part of the speech concentrates on showing the existence of a problem, and the second part shows how a particular course of action will solve the problem. Such a speech usually leans heavily to information, so marshaled as to demonstrate the existence and extent of the problem and the capacity of the proposed solution to solve it. Generally the audience is made acquainted with only a single solution (the one the speaker wants to advocate) and criteria for an acceptable solution are assumed to be those that can be inferred from the speaker's reasoning.

When audience commitment and action can be obtained quickly enough that an opposition will not have time to crystallize, a speech of the type just described has some chance of success. On the other hand, if the action that is asked of the listeners will be delayed, then an opposition will have time to form and present counter-arguments and alternative solutions. Then for that audience the entire process of arriving at a decision probably will involve the acquisition of information and a consideration of alternative solutions and of criteria for evaluation of solutions. In that case, the speaker must decide whether to touch upon these issues in outlining his solution or to limit his presentation to a description of the problem, leaving the solution stage to later persuasive efforts by himself or others.

**How has the audience formulated the problem?** Opportunities to speak to audiences that are entirely unaware of the speaker's problem are rather rare. On the other hand, it is fairly common for a speaker to confront an audience that is aware that some problem exists, but has either failed to formulate the problem clearly or has formulated it in a way that is incompatible with the speaker's understanding of the problem. In the previous example of the forest traveler, for instance, it makes considerable difference whether the traveler says, "I will have to find some way to get past this tree," or "I must find some way to get around this tree," or "I must find a way to get over this tree," or "I must find some way to move this tree out of the way." Each of these formulations of the problem favors certain courses of action and ignores others.

In the same way, an audience is predisposed to consider different courses of action with respect to civil rights demonstrations if a speaker says, "We must pacify these people," or "We must find some way to meet the needs of these protesting groups," or "We must find some way to get these agitators out of the streets," or "We must find more effective means of controlling these outbursts," or "We must find some way of showing these people the futility of their actions." Each formulation of the problem represents a different way of looking at the situation and determines in part the approach to a solution. If most of the audience has formulated the problem in some way that is incompatible with the line of thinking that the speaker wants to develop, he may find it essential to get the audience to reformulate the problem in their own minds before he can proceed any further. Indeed, he may find that this reformulation is all he can hope for in a single speech.

**How much information does the audience have?** An auditor may be conscious of some supposed problem and may even have formulated it in explicit terms, yet still have relatively little information about it. In fact, he may have taken a position with respect to a preferred course of action without having much information on which to base his judgment. In planning for communication, the speaker needs to take account of the information that his auditors already have.

In deciding whether to present information relative to the problem, the speaker is confronted with conflicting demands. On one hand, it is inefficient to present information to an audience that has it already and doing so may irritate some auditors. On the other hand, it is generally ineffective to recommend a course of action to an auditor until he has enough information to serve as a basis of opinion formation or change. If the listener does not have the information that would support a decision, then it may be the speaker's most important function to provide it.

As we shall see later in the chapter, the difference between the informed and the uninformed auditor must be considered in connection with the question of whether the auditor has taken a position on the speaker's proposal. The informed-hostile audience presents a different problem to the speaker than the uninformed-hostile one, and the informed-neutral is a different sort of auditor from the uninformed-neutral. Thus, the amount of information possessed by an auditor does not of itself provide a reliable foundation for a strategy of communication; but taken in connection with other facts about the listener, the amount of information he holds relevant to the problem in question is an important variable in determining how various kinds of communication are likely to affect him, and in particular how important it is that specific items of information be presented in the speech.

**Has the auditor considered alternate courses of action?** At first glance it may appear that the listener who is well-informed about a problem will also have considered most of the possible solutions to it, but the fact is quite otherwise.

We have already noted that individuals do not necessarily follow the stages of the reflective thinking process in the order that Dewey described as ideal. Very often a person collects most of his information about a problem **after he has already decided how it should be solved.**

The suspension of judgment required to follow the reflective thinking process in its ideal order is extremely difficult to achieve. Ordinarily, as soon as we become aware of a problem we begin looking for solutions to it. Most of us dislike unfinished business, and an unsolved problem—that is, a problem to which we have not thought of an acceptable solution—is unfinished business. It is as if the problem, once recognized, continues to press upon our thoughts until we find what appears to be a workable solution to it. Having thought of such a solution, the mind is set at rest, and having established a satisfactory state of mind, a person is resistant to any forces that would tend to reopen the issue.

The tendency to jump to a solution and then to resist further consideration of other alternatives seems to vary somewhat from one person to another, but most individuals have a rather low tolerance for ambiguity and dislike indecisiveness. Therefore they not only tend to reach a conclusion as quickly as possible, but having reached it once, they are loath to relinquish it. Moreover, they tend to seek out information about the issue that is consistent with the stand they have already taken. This leads in turn to a tendency to select communication sources and channels that support the listener's own position. Thus a person may accumulate a great store of information from a limited range of sources, all of it supporting a single viewpoint or proposed solution to the problem. Other information, which might have caused him to consider alternative proposals, may be effectively screened out. Under these circumstances the listener is likely to feel that his conviction is based on information—whereas in fact just the reverse is true; his information is based on conviction.

On those occasions when a person considers alternate courses of action after he has already made up his mind about the problem, the usual outcome of such consideration is a phenomenon called "inoculation." In its normal medical usage, "inoculation" refers to the procedure of introducing disease germs in a weakened state into the blood stream, causing the body to develop antibodies. If a virulent form of the disease subsequently should enter the body, its defenses will be mobilized and the disease germs destroyed. The term is used analogously in communication to refer to the process of introducing counterarguments, opposing viewpoints, or alternative courses of action in a weak form, then denying or refuting them. The inoculation theory holds that this procedure makes the listener more resistant to the same arguments when they are subsequently presented to him in stronger form.

The listener who has been inoculated—or who has inoculated himself—in this fashion against a particular line of argument is likely to be particularly resistant to attitude or opinion change. He therefore represents a particular challenge and a somewhat different problem from the listener who has not been exposed at all. The listener who has considered your solution and rejected it, even though the grounds of his rejection may be inadequate, is more difficult to persuade than the listener who has never considered it at all.

**What criteria will the audience apply?** The criteria that we apply to determining the best solution to a problem often exert a powerful but subconscious influence on our thinking. Such criteria, for example, probably are the most significant features separating opposed political philosophies.

For instance, history probably will show that the American conservative of the 1960's (regardless of political party) probably differed from the typical liberal of the same period largely on the basis of the criteria that each applied to proposed solutions for social and economic problems. In general (contrary to a popular view) both were aware of general problems, even though they phrased them differently. In general, the leaders of both groups were well-informed. Both had considered essentially the same range of possible solutions. But the two groups differed radically with respect to criteria to be applied in selecting a solution; indeed, on crucial points their criteria were almost perfectly opposed. For example, the liberal's philosophy provided that planning be done on the grandest possible scale; preferably at the federal level. For the conservative, any solution that expanded government, especially at the federal level, was unacceptable; planning should be done on the smallest possible scale, preferably at the level of the individual. Agreement with respect to government policy between such opposed viewpoints would be extremely difficult, for most programs acceptable to one would be completely unacceptable to the other.

As the foregoing example illustrates, the criteria that an auditor is prepared to apply to any proposed solution to a problem play a significant role in his decision-making processes. It follows that they also play a significant role in his reaction to communication designed to analyze a problem or recommend a course of action.

**Has the audience committed itself on the question?** In designing a strategy of communication for analyzing a problem or recommending a course of action, the single factor that most speakers want to know about is whether the listener has already made up his mind about the question, and if so what his position is. The reason for this concern, of course, is that the committed listener approaches the speech situation in a frame of mind that is entirely different from that of the uncommitted listener, and the listener who is committed in favor of a proposition approaches the situation differently from the listener who is committed against it.

Of much greater importance is the question of why the listener is committed one way or the other, or why he has failed to take a stand on the question. Consider three listeners: one is undecided because he has never thought about the question; a second is undecided because he cannot choose between two courses of action that seem equally attractive to him; and the third is undecided because all of the possibilities seem equally bad. From the standpoint of their receptiveness to communications of various kinds, these three listeners differ from one another markedly, even though all three are uncommitted.

In applying the reflective thinking process to audience analysis, it is important to know not just whether the auditor is committed and in what direction, but how much and what kind of reflective thinking has preceded his commitment. The state of his commitment is most useful for telling us how he stands at the moment; if we are to predict how he will respond to various patterns of communication, we shall need to know not just where he stands but how he got there.

**Reflective thinking and the auditor group.** It is not characteristic of individual decision-making to withhold judgment until all of the facts are in and all of the possible courses of action have been considered. Ordinarily as soon as a person has enough information at hand to give some shape to a problem, he casts about for a solution and usually settles on the first one encountered which seems reasonable. On the other hand, because of diversity of background and viewpoint, groups and assemblies usually do a more adequate job of defining the problem, gathering information, considering alternative courses of action, and formulating criteria for selecting the preferred solution. That is, groups usually do a more thorough job of reflective thinking than do individuals.

For this reason, when advocating a course of action or speaking about a problem, it is important for the speaker to know to what extent the issue has been discussed among the members of his audience. The more they have talked with one another (or been exposed to the same communications from outside the group) the more alike their thinking will be, and the further developed their thinking is likely to be in terms of the reflective thinking process. And the more thoroughly developed their thinking is, the more important it is for the speaker to know how they have formulated the problem, what information they have, what alternatives they have considered, what criteria they have established for an acceptable solution, and the extent to which they have committed themselves to support a particular course of action.

With this information in hand, the speaker is in a much better position to formulate a strategy of communication. He can select his specific objective in light of what seems possible and desirable, and he can select speech content calculated to move the audience from where it is toward where he would like it to be.

# SEVEN

# Auditor opinion as a basis for analysis

To the speaker who sees his ultimate goal as the promulgation of some attitude or behavior, it is essential to know the position of his auditors with respect to that attitude or behavior. If he cannot know their position directly, he will try to infer it from surrounding circumstances and from other information about them.

**Partisans, neutrals, and opponents.** The speaker's first inclination probably will be to divide his auditors into three broad groups: partisans, neutrals, and opponents. If we refer to the speaker's recommended attitude or behavior as the "proposition," then partisans are those who support the proposition, opponents are those who stand against it, and neutrals are those whose position is either undetermined or ambiguous. Such a division provides the speaker with some rough guidelines in selecting a specific purpose and content for the speech, and some basis for predicting responses and subsequent behavior of auditor groups.

A partisan auditor speaks favorably of the proposition and, if a vote were taken, would vote in favor of it. With respect to such an auditor, the speaker probably will see his major objective as maintaining the partisan's enthusiasm and strengthening his commitment to the proposition. If forces are at work in the community that would generate counterarguments to which the partisan might be exposed, the speaker may concentrate some of his attention on means for inoculating the partisan against these counterarguments. In planning for communication to partisans, the speaker is inclined to predict that such an auditor will accept the speaker's information without hesitation, will not examine his logical arguments with an overly critical eye, and will be ready to respond emotionally to images and concepts favorable to the proposition.

An opponent auditor speaks unfavorably of the proposition and, if a vote were taken, would vote against it. The speaker generally will recognize the futility of trying to convert an opponent to a partisan by means of a single speech. Instead, his strategy usually will be at most to neutralize the opponent or to weaken his commitment. If the opposing attitude is well-entrenched, the speaker may feel that he can do no more than raise doubts about certain ideas or arguments which support the opposing attitude; and if the opposition is violent, he may sense that the most he can accomplish is to reduce the intensity of the opposing attitude. He will be aware of the danger of a "boomerang" effect if he asks for too great an attitude change with such an auditor. The speaker may predict that this auditor will demand documentation and proof for information supporting the proposition, that he will subject the speaker's logical arguments to very critical analysis in an effort to find logical flaws, and that any attempt to involve his emotions will meet with a hostile reaction. If he changes at all, it will be as a result of accepting new information or seeing some aspect of the proposition from a new perspective.

It is when we come to the neutral auditor that we see most clearly that the division of auditors into partisan, opponent, and neutral groups is a consequence of approaching the analysis of audience attitude from the point of view of an election, in which the auditor has three choices: to vote for the proposition (or candidate), to vote against the proposition (or candidate), or to abstain from voting. Within this framework, most speakers feel they can have their greatest impact on the neutral auditor. While it is important to keep all of the "yes" votes, and to win as many as possible of the "no" votes (or at least to change them to abstentions), the major opportunity in an election campaign lies with the neutrals, for partisans and opponents are hard to change, and in most elections there are enough neutrals to swing the outcome one way or the other.

Most analysts would divide neutrals into two groups: informed-neutrals and uninformed-neutrals. The informed-neutral is rare. He speaks about the proposition in both favorable and unfavorable terms, and if a vote were taken he probably would abstain. The speaker usually recognizes the unlikelihood of converting this auditor with a single speech. He will see his major opportunity for influence in the possibility of strengthening conviction on those points favorable to the proposition and weakening barriers to acceptance of other points. In planning speech content, he will anticipate that the informed-neutral will have some doubt concerning the accuracy of the speaker's information, some suspicion about the rigor of his logic, and will be wary of emotional involvement. In anticipation of these attitudes and expectations, the speaker ordinarily will build a speech around information and analysis, documenting information accurately, demonstrating logical soundness, and choosing emotional appeals with care, while seeking to avoid the impression of rabid partisanship. Where he can do so without damaging his own case, he will admit opposing arguments to demonstrate that he, too, can see both sides of the question

The uninformed-neutral is the unsmelted gold of the election campaign and a prime target for communicators of all kinds. He is the **tabula rasa** on whom the persuaders of both sides hope to place their mark. It is possible to convert him to partisanship or opposition with a single speech. The speaker will recognize in him an original lack of interest in the proposition and the need for information and for a clear-cut and thorough delineation of the issues. The speaker will plan a communication that first will enlist interest, then give the auditor the information he needs for opinion formation, and finally interpret this information in a way favorable to the proposition. If the opposition is strong or growing, he may plan to inoculate the uninformed-neutral auditor against major opposing arguments.

**The microstructure of opinion.** The foregoing analysis asks for the auditor's attitude toward a single item, the proposition itself. But the proposition does not stand alone; it is embedded in a matrix of other statements, some of which tend to support and some of which tend to oppose it. For example, the proposition "We should pull the Marines out of Viet Nam" would **tend** to be supported by such statements as "The presence of U.S. troops in Viet Nam is a source of resentment among oriental peoples," and "It is morally wrong to intervene in the political affairs of another nation." The same proposition would **tend** to be opposed by such statements as "The presence of U.S. troops in Viet Nam is a bulwark against Communism," and "We would lose face by withdrawing from Viet Nam at this time." To know how an auditor responds to each of these and similar related statements, over and beyond how he responds to the proposition itself, adds considerable detail to the understanding of the auditor's position.

In exposing the microstructure of an auditor's opinion, the analyst will seek to determine which statements related to the proposition the auditor agrees with (the **acceptance set**), which statements he disagrees with (the **rejection set**), and which statements he does not care about (the **indifference set**).

Consider, for example, the following proposition and related statements:

Proposition:  We should adopt a system of socialized medicine in the United States.

Statements:   A. Many poor people are unable to pay for medical care.
              B. Socialized medicine has worked in Sweden.
              C. We all have a responsibility to care for persons who are in need.
              D. The cost of medical care would rise under socialized medicine.
              E. The record-keeping required for socialized medicine would lead to an invasion of privacy.
              F. Socialism results in loss of personal initiative.

In general, statements A, B, and C tend to support the proposition; that is, unless discounted by some qualification, acceptance of A, B, and C predisposes an auditor toward socialized medicine. Conversely, statements D, E, and F tend to oppose the proposition; that is, these statements are characteristic of the opinions of persons who oppose socialized medicine.

In general, for strong partisans the acceptance set of relevant statements will be found to contain mostly statements tending to support the proposition; the rejection set of relevant statements will contain mostly statements tending to oppose the proposition; and the indifference set of relevant statements will contain very few statements. (For instance, if the six statements above composed for a given partisan auditor the set of relevant statements, then the first three would probably fall in the acceptance set, the last three in the rejection set, and the indifference set would be empty.) On the other hand, for strong opponents the acceptance set of relevant statements will be found to contain mostly statements tending to oppose the proposition, the rejection set of relevant statements will contain mostly statements tending to support the proposition, and the indifference set of relevant statements will contain few or no statements. (For the extreme opponent of socialized medicine, the first three statements would fall in the rejection set, the last three in the acceptance set, and the indifference set would be empty.)

However, for most propositions the groups of strong partisans and strong opponents will be relatively small; these are the extremists who have organized their thinking to an inordinate degree around the proposition in question. Most partisans will be found to accept some statements tending to oppose the proposition and to reject some statements tending to support the proposition; and most opponents will be found to reject some statements tending to oppose the proposition and to accept some statements tending to support the proposition. (For instance, an auditor might agree with statements B, C, and D, be indifferent to E, disagree with A and F, and support socialized medicine—or oppose it.)

When we speak of the set of relevant statements, of course, we are not talking about relevance in an absolute, logical, or omniscient sense; we use the term "relevant" to refer to those statements that the auditor himself judges to be connected in some way with the proposition. Consequently, for the informed auditor, especially one who has been exposed to considerable argument on the proposition, the set of relevant statements is extremely large; if the auditor is very well versed on the question, his set of relevant statements may contain most of the statements that are relevant in a logical sense to the proposition. On the other hand, the uninformed auditor will have a set of relevant statements that is quite small.

As the auditor is exposed to communication, the set of relevant statements will grow in two ways: (1) Some statements which the auditor did not previously have in his repertoire will be added by the communicator (i.e., he will learn some entirely new facts and concepts that bear on the proposition). (2) Some statements that he already had in his repertoire but had not previously associated with the proposition will come into association (i.e., his previous knowledge will be brought to bear on the question). In other words, the set of relevant statements is expanded by adding information and by showing the relevance of known facts and opinions.

It is the existence of some inconsistency within the microstructure of most auditors' opinions, coupled with the possibility of expanding the set of relevant statements, that makes possible opinion change on controversial questions. As we have seen, with the exception of the uninformed-neutral, the likelihood of producing dramatic opinion change on a controversial topic through a single speech is very small; but it is possible to produce some change in the opinion microstructure by emphasizing those relevant statements that tend to support the speaker's proposition, by adding new information to the acceptance and rejection sets of relevant statements, and by adding to the acceptance and rejection sets through demonstrating the relevance of previously-known statements tending to support the proposition. In order to accomplish these objectives, the speaker needs to know not just how the auditor stands with respect to the proposition, but also what he knows and how he thinks about questions related to it. Over a long period of time, small increments produced through judicious use of such knowledge can culminate in a substantial change of attitude or opinion.

**Extrinsic vs. intrinsic grounds.** A second feature that is overlooked by the division of auditors into partisan, neutral, and opponent groups is the question of **why** the auditor falls into one group or the other. In examining opinion microstructure, the analyst is concerned largely with what we may call intrinsic considerations; but it makes considerable difference in response to communication whether the auditor has reached his position on such intrinsic grounds or, on the contrary, has come to his position through the intervention of extrinsic factors.

An auditor's position on a proposition may be said to be based on **intrinsic** grounds to the extent that his position rests upon facts, arguments, or issues that, in his mind, are directly related to the acceptability of the proposition itself. His position may be said to be based on **extrinsic** grounds to the extent that it rests upon factors that, in his mind, are not directly related to the acceptability of the proposition, but are related to the acceptability of taking a certain position on it. This distinction may be sharpened by considering an example: You may contribute to the annual office Community Chest drive because you want to see local charities prosper. Because the prosperity of local charities is related directly in your mind to contributing to the Community Chest, your grounds in this case are intrinsic. On the other hand, a fellow worker may contribute because he does not wish to appear miserly or callous to his superior who has asked for the contribution. In this instance, his decision to contribute is based on the poor image that he expects to have if he refuses, and not on any inherent desirability of contributing; thus his grounds are extrinsic.

To the mass persuader looking for ways to influence the attitudes and behaviors of large groups of people, extrinsic and intrinsic avenues of approach are equally valuable. The National Education Association, for example, appeals to individual teachers in its membership drives by pointing out the great advantages of membership to the individual. At the same time, the NEA awards recognition to schools with 100 per cent membership on their faculties, thus assuring that superintendents, principals, and colleagues will bring extrinsic pressures to bear on individuals for whom the intrinsic arguments are ineffectual. The combination of intrinsic and extrinsic approaches is extremely potent. Actually, in choosing among possible approaches to mass persuasion, the distinction between the two is often unimportant.

However, when analyzing the grounds of an auditor's position on a proposition, the distinction between extrinsic and intrinsic grounds is significant. The committed auditor, whether partisan, neutral or opponent, who has reached his position on intrinsic grounds is likely to be informed about the facts and aware of the major lines of argument habitually cited on both sides of the question. He is less likely to be taken off guard by new arguments, will have developed through inoculation and counterargument ways of disposing of major opposing arguments, and thus will be able to defend his commitment if it is challenged. On the other hand, the committed auditor who has come to his position on extrinsic grounds is likely to have much less information about the facts related to the proposition, is more likely to be taken off guard by new arguments because he is not acquainted with the issues, will have weak defenses against counterarguments, and thus will be less able to defend his commitment if it is challenged.

Ordinarily, both extrinsic commitment and intrinsic commitment lead to an increased interest in the proposition, with the result that the committed auditor seeks out communication supporting his viewpoint and tends to screen out communication opposing it. However, the way in which this interest and consequent selection operate is different for those with a primarily extrinsic and those with a primarily intrinsic base for commitment. The basis of this difference lies in the fact that the set of relevant statements is much larger for the auditor with an intrinsically-based commitment. Thus he is able to relate more of what he sees and hears about the proposition to information and attitudes that he already has.

Finally, the auditor who has reached commitment on intrinsic grounds will have attained some measure of internal harmony and consistency in the microstructure of his ideas and beliefs surrounding the topic. As we noted in considering the reflective thinking process, this state of internal balance will make it difficult to introduce to him any contradictory elements, for contrary facts and arguments will be inconsistent with what he already knows and believes. He will demand meticulous proof of any alleged facts that could be used to undermine his conviction, and he will be strongly motivated to look for logical flaws in counter-arguments.

On the other hand, the auditor who is commited largely on extrinsic grounds may have no well-balanced view of the proposition; indeed, on intrinsic grounds he may find it altogether objectionable. Many thousands of people each year contribute to causes and pay dues to organizations with which they have no sympathy or to which they are opposed in principle, but which they support in order to retain some privilege or to avoid the disapproval of others. The opinion microstructure of such an auditor is of interest to both partisan and opponent speakers; his acceptance set may contain many statements tending to oppose the proposition, and his rejection set may contain many statements tending to favor the proposition.

If extrinsic grounds of commitment are strong, opposing communications may have little immediate effect upon this auditor; thus, in most elections and other short-term campaigns it is not usually thought worthwhile to address much communication to such auditors—for partisans they are safe, and for opponents they are out of reach, because the grounds of commitment are not such as to be responsive to argument on the issues. Moreover, listening to communication on either side of the proposition may be uncomfortable for such an auditor because it brings into focus the discrepancy between his beliefs and his actions. Thus, the partisan speaker may feel that it is best to let sleeping anxieties lie and the opponent speaker may realize that such an auditor will make strong efforts to avoid receiving his messages.

Sometimes an extrinsically-committed auditor cannot avoid receiving opposing messages. On these occasions, the fact that he does not shift manifest opinion does not mean that the messages have no effect. Indeed, they may have a profound effect on the opinion microstructure, making the auditor in effect a turncoat-in-embryo, who requires only a weakening of the extrinsic grounds of commitment for conversion to the opposing side of the proposition.

We have spoken of the grounds of commitment largely in terms of the partisan and opponent auditor, but the same principle may be used to differentiate committed neutrals into those who are committed on intrinsic and those who are committed on extrinsic grounds.

It is important first to make the distinction between committed and uncommitted neutrals. The uncommitted neutral is the only type of auditor who may be said to have no position on the proposition. He is neutral because he is uninterested in the question or because he is unacquainted with facts and arguments required to form an opinion. The committed neutral, however, has a very definite position on the proposition: the position of neutrality. He has thought about the proposition and has decided neither to oppose nor to support it. The important point is that committed neutrality is a position from which it is at least as difficult to win an auditor as either partisanship or opposition.

If the neutral's commitment is based on extrinsic considerations, he usually believes that he stands to lose something by joining either side, and so has taken himself out of the issue. He will seek to avoid communication on either side. On the other hand, if the neutral's commitment is based on intrinsic considerations, he finds equal merit and/or defect in both partisan and opponent positions. He will be open to communication from both sides but will be skeptical of both.

One final point needs to be made concerning the bases of opinion. Although an auditor may initially adopt a position of partisanship, neutrality, or opposition for extrinsic reasons, ordinarily he will make some effort to find good reasons with which to provide for himself and others the appearance of intrinsic commitment; that is, he will usually try to rationalize his position. For such an auditor, the most important function of the partisan speaker is to provide him with the rationalizations he needs to maintain the appearance of reasonableness. Until a solid structure of such rationalization has been built, the extrinsically-committed auditor is in an unstable condition and potentially persuasible if the extrinsic ground of commitment can be weakened.

# Selected bibliography

Andersen, Martin P., Wesley Lewis, and James Murray, **The Speaker and His Audience.** New York: Harper & Row, 1964. Chapter 3, "Understanding Your Listeners," deals with factors affecting individual listening behavior and group influences on the individual. Chapter 8, "Analyzing the Audience and Occasion," describes a representative procedure for audience preanalysis based on demographic characteristics. Supplements Chapters 1, 2, and 3.

Auer, J. Jeffery, **An Introduction to Research in Speech.** New York: Harper & Brothers, 1959. Chapter VI, "The Descriptive Method," beginning with Part II, "Sampling," discusses sampling, observational techniques, questionnaire construction, interview procedures, and scaling devices. Supplements Chapter 4.

Berlo, David K., **The Process of Communication.** New York: Holt, Rinehart and Winston, 1960. Chapter 6, "Social Systems," deals with the influence of group factors on individual behavior and with the predictability of auditor response from knowledge of group characteristics and habits. Supplements, especially, Chapter 2.

Boulding, Kenneth E., **The Image.** Ann Arbor: The University of Michigan Press, 1961. The subtitle of this book, "Knowledge in Life and Society," suggests its content. "The Image" is

119

discussed as an integrating factor in knowledge and behavior. Chapters IV, "The Image of Man and Society"; V, "The Public Image and the Sociology of Knowledge"; VII, "The Image in the Political Process"; and IX, "Subcultures and the Subuniverses of Discourse," are especially interesting. Supplements Chapter 5.

Bryant, Donald C., and Karl R. Wallace, **Fundamentals of Public Speaking** (Third Ed.). New York: Appleton-Century-Crofts, 1960. Chapters 18, "The Audience: Motives and Basic Lines of Thought," and 19, "The Audience: Partisans, Neutrals, Opponents," present a scheme for analyzing and adapting to audience predispositions in preparing persuasive speeches. Supplements Chapter 7.

Cronkhite, Gary Lynn, "Logic, Emotion, and the Paradigm of Persuasion," **Quarterly Journal of Speech,** L, No. 1, discusses persuasion that calls for analysis of issues on the basis of audience beliefs and values. Although not intended as a basis for audience analysis, the states of the auditor are treated as basic to the influence of persuasive discourse, and the reader may develop from the elements of the persuasion paradigm a scheme for audience analysis. Supplements Part II, especially Chapter 7.

Deutschmann, Paul J., "Measurement in Communication Research," in **Introduction to Mass Communication Research,** eds. Ralph O. Nafziger and David M. White. Baton Rouge: Louisiana State University Press, 1958. A description of some general types of measurement that are often useful in audience analysis. Supplements Chapter 4.

Eisenson, Jon, J. Jeffery Auer, and John V. Irwin, **The Psychology of Communication.** New York: Appleton-Century-Crofts, 1963. Chapter 16, "Psychology of Public Address," presents a summary of more than 100 experimental findings concerning the influence of various factors in the speech-communication situation upon audience response. Supplements Chapters 2 and 3.

Kraus, Sidney, ed., **The Great Debates.** Bloomington: University of Indiana Press, 1962. Part II, "Effects of the Debates," presents the results of several studies designed to measure the impact of the Kennedy-Nixon Presidential election debates of 1960 upon public opinion concerning the issues and candidates. Supplements Chapters 3 and 4.

Woolbert, Charles H., "The Audience," **Psychological Monographs** (June, 1916), 37–54. One of the earliest and to this day one of the most cogent treatments of the major factors operating to shape response in large, orderly, group-conscious assemblages operating with a common focus of attention. Supplements Part I, especially Chapter 1.

# Index

123

Process of abstraction, 18
Process of speech communication, 3
Product effects and responses, 41, 64
Program analysis, 6
  (**see** audience analyzers)
Program analyzer, 61
  (**see** audience analyzer)
Programmed textbooks, 37
Proportion, 19
Psychological set, 40
Public information or persuasion programs, 25
Public-speaking classrooms, 34
Public support, 34
Pupillary dilation, 39
Purpose, 23, 24, 27, 42, 45, 49
  limitation of, 35
  subsidiary purpose, 47
Purpose-oriented analysis, 44, 51
Quasi-quantitative concepts, 17, 18
Quasi-statistical concepts, 18
Questionnaires, 67–68
Random sample, 76
Range, 21
Rational decisions, 100
Rational explanations, 95
Rationalization, 118
Recognition test, 71
Recorded lecture, 37
Reflective thinking and the auditor group, 108
Reflective thinking process, 100
  definition of problem, 101
  felt need or difficulty, 101
  identifying criteria for solution, 101

Reflective thinking process (cont.)
  listing alternate solutions, 101
  (**see** problem-solution sequence)
Rejection set, 112
Relevance, 113
Relevant statements, set of, 116
  acceptance set, 112
  indifference set, 112
  rejection set, 112
Representative audience members, 45
  (**see** officers)
Representativeness of measures, 21
Response readiness, 12
Retransmission, 33
Routine, 23, 100
Salience, 85, 90, 96
Salience v. valuation, 85
Samples, 76
  (**see** inference from samples)
Satisfaction, 39
Secondary communicators, 33
Selection of specific purpose, 35
Selective exposure, 106, 116
Semantic differential, 68
Sense impressions, 81
Situational factors, 28
Skin temperature, 73
Small groups, 9
Speaker, 3, 25
Speaker-centered approaches to communication, 4
Speaker's freedom to choose topic, 34
Statistical approach, 14, 40, 55–56, 63